Fish and Chips with Batter Bits

Angela Parkes

Many thanks to the Black Country Bugle for their kind help in this project

Dedicated to everyone who
keeps the memories
alive.

My sincere thanks to:

Catherine Flavell
Sydney Parkes
Dorothy Turley

Contents

52°32′N 2°2′W / 52.533°N 2.033°W / 52.533; -2.033.

Introduction

Ow bist thee? Ow bin ya? How are you? Welcome to Black Country food.

Sitting in the heart of the Midlands, in its heyday the Black Country was an industrial region populated by chain makers, nail makers, miners, foundry men and forgers. Slag heaps of black spoil and coal dust covered the land, skies blackened with the smoke that belched from chimneys, faces black with the grime earned from hard toil. After dark, the fires of the forges and the glow of molten metal lit the sky. The American consul to Birmingham, Elihu Burritt coined the phrase "black by day, red by night" in a now iconic description of the Black Country.

To declare the Black Country as industrial is beyond doubt, but the exact location is harder to define. West of Birmingham, and including Dudley, Tipton, Old Hill, parts of Walsall, possibly Sandwell, but not Wolverhampton, probably, or Birmingham, definitely. The boundaries may lie five miles from Dudley Castle, or those places within an hour's weary trudge of the castle walls. It may be where coal seam runs close to the surface or Queen Victoria may have named the region when her train passed through. Henry VIII was given credit referring to the Blacke Countrie where coal coloured the ground.

So it would seem we are not entirely sure exactly which areas the Black Country includes, or how it acquired the name. The debate is long and heated and not for finishing here, but one thing is certain; the Black Country is where you will find a Black Country Mon

It was hard to find enough traditional Black Country recipes to fill a book and those included are not all exclusive to the region, though many may have originated here. What they do have in common is that the people have enjoyed them.

Behind each traditional recipe is a story, several stories, as they pass from generation to generation. Fond memories are stored in those recipes. Except, often there were no recipes, there was no written track, cooking was from instinct - a dash of that, a pinch of this, a tweak here, a tweak there. Chuck it in today, it will have gone off by tomorrow cooking. With each generation that passed more knowledge vanished. This is an attempt to chronicle some of these recipes before they are lost forever, but as the research was done, it became clear that it was already too late, a lot of what should be remembered was already gone, half memories battered by time were sometimes all that survived.

Times were often hard and money short, the food reflected that. One school of thought holds that preserving the past, simply because of its heritage is of no merit; tastes change and time moves on. However, the reason these recipes have survived is because people enjoy them and that makes them worth preserving. In addition, they are also part of the social history, the very fabric of the region.

Cast iron cooking pots bubbled in kitchens from Coseley to Roseville, Cradley to Old Hill, producing belly-filling stodge. Pigs, not fairies lived at the bottom of the garden and hops grew on wires to feed the brew houses. Here are some recipes from an age that is gone, along with the foundry men, coal miners, boatmen or chain makers who ate the food. Black Country folk may be renowned for being rough and ready, but they were and they remain the salt of the earth, hearts as big as buckets.

Although the food was often high in fat and sugar, there was no obesity crisis here generations ago – because the people worked and they worked hard. It was the blood, sweat and toil of the men who built and worked the mills and the mines, the factories and the foundries of the Black Country; but it was the women who fed them.

So cook it while you can – it's bostin' fittle as they say in the Black Country.

The Kitchen is the heart of the home

"Nan lived in Coseley. I was only six or seven when she passed away, so memories of the kitchen are only fragments. I remember the cold feel of the red quarry tiles on bare feet; I remember the smell of the kitchen cupboards, the door to the garden that led out through the scullery. I remember picking ripe strawberries in the back garden and eating them in the sun, washing vegetables fresh from the soil in the white, oblong Belfast sink, but little else. I remember the fire grate in the living room but I don't remember the food, not a single meal. If she were alive now, Nan's memories would go back as far as the late 1800's. Times have changed so much and there's so much I wish I could ask."

Family life is often played out in the kitchen, even now. In the era before microwaves, ready meals and dishwashers, so much more time was spent there, a warm fire in winter, and the welcoming smell of cooking food, the kitchen truly was the heart of the home. But the rosy glow of nostalgia can be deceiving, the labour was hard, no dishwashers or automatic washing machines. An ash filled grate to clear out and fire to light before the cooking could start.

The forerunner of refrigerators was a cold shelf in the pantry, hidden in the shaded depths and on which butter, cream or cold meats were stored. A thick, slab three or four inches thick, some had marble tops, others had tiles. Even in summer these were cool the touch, and in the days before fridges, these simple innovations did much to prolong the shelf life of foods that now we would automatically place in the fridge.

"Dad used to call his mother's house in Meadow Lane, the Cott. Although memories of this are fading now, some remain buried deep, just accessible as I walk through the house that now only exists stored in the cells of living brains and as each cell ceases to exist so a little more is lost to the mists of time."

Beginning to disappear rapidly from living memory are the cooking methods of yesteryear. Generally, grates were of the black lead type, elbow grease and black lead paste kept them pristine. The fire was the main method of cooking, over or in front of the fire itself, or the heat from the fire warmed an oven set into the fireplace, next to the fire hole. Some of these ovens were quite large.

Poking the fire with a long metal poker would break up the lumps of coal to make it burn better and riddling the ashes through into the ashtray underneath allowed the air to be drawn up and the fire burn hotter. The tray would fill up until the gap narrowed between the bottom of the fire and the tray, choking the fire. Emptying it was a dusty job; ash would get into the nose and throat and leave a layer of dust on the mantle.

To one side was an oven with the hob on top, heated by the fire. Effective, but learning to gauge the temperature led to interesting results. The oven needed time to warm and its temperature was more stable when the coals had settled to a steady red glow. In the winter with careful management, the fire could be left in overnight and a little coaxing the following morning would be all that was needed for it to spring back to life, this kept the hob and oven ticking over, otherwise there would be a half hour wait for the kettle to boil for the first cup of tea. On the other side of the fire from the oven there may have been nothing, or another oven or possibly a hot water boiler with a tap.

In front and to the side of the fire would be an assortment of racks and hooks to hang various contraptions including a Dutch oven or there may have been meat jacks to hang the meat near the fire to roast. The heat would cause this to rotate gently or an operative would turn this during the cooking process, similar to a rotisserie, producing wonderfully flavoured succulent results. A pan or tray underneath would catch the dripping and meat juices to dip in later. Almost every house had one of the large, black enamelled cooking pots somewhere on the premises; latterly these were often used for a variety of purposes not including cooking. Examples such as collecting engine oil as it drains out of the engine, a container to stir paint in, collecting garden weeds or as a planter, but sadly not for boiling up hearty soups or stews.

The Dutch oven was not an oven at all, but a hanging metal open tin placed in front of the fire. Meat or bacon hung on the hooks and bathed in the heat from the flames. The heat was also reflected from the back of the Dutch oven onto the meat, cooking it from both sides. Glistening fat ran down the meat, dripping into the tray below, pieces of bread were dipped in for a tasty treat; or the fat was poured out into a cup or other suitable container and saved to be used later.

Lighting the fire was an art form, a knack. On days when the coal making up the fire was poor quality or the wind was in the wrong direction, the fire would not draw, the oven would take forever to warm up or worse still smoke would billow back down the chimney filling the kitchen. Many a cold morning was spent sitting in front of the hearth with a sheet of newspaper held across the opening to get the fire to draw, followed by squeals and yelps when it did, sucked the paper in and set it alight like the Bonanza map.

Sugar came in loaves; customers bought salt carved from huge solid blocks delivered by horse and cart, such as the round that delivered to Gornal, locals bought only what they needed, no more no less. Cheese was cut to size with a wire, tea came loose not in bags, weighed out by the quarter and slid into oblong parcels deftly created from sheets of flat paper in front of your eyes and tied up with string.

"The smell of wooden kitchen cupboards mixed with damp brings back memories of standing on a stool at nans worktop, fingers caked in rock bun mix. A hotchpotch of the memories that make up childhood all jumbled together"

Gardens were larger, playing a more important role than a place to put the barbeque and display the decking. There would be flowers in the summer, dahlias and roses for cutting, marigolds and nasturtiums for colour, bushes at the corners of the lawn, privet hedges marking out the boundary. Like everything else, the garden worked, providing an area to supplement the diet. Most houses had a productive vegetable patch to supply the table. In addition, there would often be soft fruits and rhubarb, together with fruit and nut trees, all providing food that changed with the seasons and produce lasting well into the winter months. Salads in the summer, potatoes mid-year, broad beans and peas for spring and early summer, brassicas – cabbage and sprouts into the winter. Strawberries, currants and gooseberries for puddings and jams.

Many a Black Country child will remember helping to dig the vegetable patch over with grandad, or picking peas for lunch and cramming more tiny sweet green balls into their mouth than they brought to the kitchen, or dipping freshly pulled rhubarb stalks in sugar.

The herb garden supplied flavour and sometimes home-medication. In the autumn there were apples and damsons for pies and chutneys. After the harvest, excess apples and pears wrapped in tissue paper were stored in a cardboard box in the cool spare room over winter, only to emerge wizened and wrinkled at regular intervals, for eating.

"Peeping over the arm of the chair, I would watch my father unwrap of one the stored apples from under the bed, unwinding the tissue paper. The skins on these little apples had yellowed and wrinkled while they were in the cardboard box. He would peel it with a butter knife. I used to watch the strand of peel getting longer as it curled away into a helix, waiting to see if the strand broke, always hoping for one long length for luck."

The house in Meadow Lane had a little square lawn at the back, with a foot wide border all the way round full of strawberry plants. To the right of this was the vegetable garden, the soil was rich; deep and well dug. Nearer to the house were thin wire frames reaching up to the sky, hop bines would race up these in summer, the hoppy smell intensifying as the cone-shaped flowers ripened.

Near to the scullery, a small Brewhouse produced gallons of beer, but again, sadly, the recollection of what was inside is very poor, although the quality of what came out was good!

At the bottom of the garden was a pigsty, as in many households they reared a pig for meat. A custom encouraged during the Second World War during meat rationing. Scraps from the table fed the animal, nothing went to waste and every bit of the pig was used.

There would have been chickens and ducks too, kept for both meat and eggs.

Duck eggs make exceedingly good cakes, deep yellow yolks impart a lovely colour to the mix and a rich flavour. The palest blue or white shells in contrast to the brown shells of the chicken eggs that are so popular today. There used to be a choice of brown or white shelled chicken eggs on sale, although the colour was different they tasted the same, white eggs are seldom found now in the UK though they are still the norm in the States.

Tales of poultry keeping abound and foxes were common in these tales, but where there is poultry there are foxes, hungry foxes. And one night when Charlie fox came to call most of the poultry at Meadow Lane met an untimely end, killed for sport rather than food, bloodied bodies left littering the grass and the path, some missing heads, others with great gaping wounds.

Only two ducks survived, one completely untouched. The other, a large white Aylesbury who was a real character and a firm favourite, was unlucky enough to have been left alive but badly mauled. The fox had ripped open the entire length of its front, leaving the breast flapping open and innards exposed. Gently the flap was repositioned and a clean towel was used to wrap the duck to secure the damage before carrying it inside complete with the hole.

What do you do with an injured duck? Damaged or not, it would still eat well and there was plenty of room in the pot. But this one was as much of a pet as a meal. Swiftly administering anaesthetic in the form of neat spirits, whisky or brandy, to numb the bird and sterilise a darning needle, the wound was sewn up. Against the odds, the bird survived and lived on for a number of years, dying eventually of natural causes.

Almost every Black Country garden had a few herbs, and it was just that, a few herbs not a formal knot garden. Fewer varieties than in the big houses and not as ornately set out, but a few plants filling a space in the corner or under the hedge.

Horseradish has been around for generations, many generations, over 3000 years and used for many things during that time, aphrodisiacs, arthritis treatments, a condiment, the applications of horseradish were many and varied.

As a relative of mustard, the hot flavour is hardly surprising, and similarly traditionally served with beef in the form of horseradish sauce. It is not the tough, spear-shaped leaves but the root, which is grated and used. When intact this has little odour, but grating releases the enzymes responsible for the familiar taste and smell.

No chicken would be complete without stuffing flavoured with sage, which also provided another use for leftover bread. The rough, green leaves were also chopped and added to faggots. Sage growing in the garden is thought to confer long life and wisdom.

Sprigs of low growing perennial thyme with its tiny green leaves were dropped into soups and stews. As evergreens, these important culinary herbs, sage and thyme were available to the cook all year round, even in deepest winter.

Moths love clothes, but they hate lavender. Small bags stuffed full of the dried herb were often one of the first needlework projects girls made at school, (this was in the days before equality of the sexes) and the fragrant pouches then hung in wardrobes and lay in drawers to scent the clothes and repel the hungry little beggars who had designs on the best woollens. Lavender also found fame as an antiseptic during the war years.

Curly leaved parsley was everywhere, rumour had it old men kept parsley seeds in their top waistcoat pocket and scattered a pinch whenever they walked the garden. The reason this took so long to germinate, and this could be weeks, was that parsley went to the devil and back seven times before its crinkled leaves poked out above the soil.

Then there was mint, the most often grown of them all. Again, it can be slow to germinate, but once it does, mint is rampant. Hardy and fast growing, frequently planted in the confines of a tin bucket to stop it spreading and taking over the garden. Tender top leaves were thrown in with new potatoes or peas as they boiled or handfuls of the fragrant herb harvested and finely chopped as the base for mint sauce. The herb aids digestion, settles the stomach, may even lower cholesterol levels and smells just beautiful. It also pairs brilliantly with lamb, cutting through the grease.

The Black Country gardens did not hold with modern designer strains of mint, none of the posh stuff, no fancy varieties. Good old fashioned garden mint with its sharp fragrance, bright green leaves and clean, refreshing taste was good enough then and is still worthy of a place in the best gardens today.

Put the maet on the bones

"Gran used to tell us this story about when she was in service. The cook had told a young girl to "put a prong in the sausage" when they opened the oven she had stuck a fork in every sausage and left them in. She used to laugh every time she told me. Which was a lot. I often wonder if that girl was Gran... She worked for the family who owned Parkes' Mill Coseley." Catherine Flavell.

Meat featured heavily in the diet, hearty appetites needed hearty food, wholesome stodge to fill the belly and fuel the hard toil that built and ran the Black Country.

Given that many households kept a customary pig at the end of the garden, the abundance of pork recipes in hardly surprising, and every bit of the pig from snout to tail was used, everything except the squeal. Nothing was wasted. Animals were useful, not only did they eat the leftovers; they converted them back into food. A plump, waste disposal unit lived in the sty at the bottom of the garden – what could be better. During the war pig bins were set up to collect scraps from the neighbourhood to feed the pigs, imagine the smell that clung to those bins on a hot summer day, it also clung to the people who emptied them, following them all day.

The sows could grow to enormous sizes, but there was a drawback, they came with a nasty bite and some with an evil temperament, especially if they had a litter of piglets. If mother pig was upset, best to know you could clear the pigsty wall in one jump because one day you might need to.

Pigs had a sixth sense, seeming to know when the end was nigh, desperate to avoid the knife they would run and the squeals when the inevitable happened would turn your stomach. Once despatched it was into hot water with the carcass to scrape off the hair. Sometimes the deadly deed occurred inside the house and afterwards, the pig went into a hot bath to be shaved.

Legend and the Black Country Bugle tell of a Mr John Longstomach, greengrocer by trade, who made his rounds by donkey cart. Tall and rake thin, he had a way with animals and a liking for ale. Something of a character if the tales are to be believed. His deliveries were often delayed, as every time he sold produce from the cart the takings would be destined for the till of the next pub on his route. The donkey, well used to the practice would gauge the stage of his master's inebriation and safely deliver him back home to his wife when he could partake no more, braying three times to announce his arrival.

Aside from the donkey, Mr Longstomach also kept a pig, a pig of whom he was fond. His other claim to fame, if local folklore is correct, was to place his pig on the wall to watch the band go by. Was it myth or was it legend? The origins of the tale are disputed and may actually lie in Dawley rather than Gornal, but Gornal will always take the fame for this. In commemoration, a stone pig still sits atop the wall in the Straits, Lower Gornal, courtesy of Roy and Janet Bradley, proudly there for all to see as they drive past.

Meat recipes abounded, some of the cheapest parts, offal such as the liver or kidneys, had the most flavour, there were many ways of cooking these and it is no wonder offal has gained so much in popularity lately.

Roasts such as beef, pork or lamb were a once a week affair and chickens, not the mass produced, plastic wrapped, cheap commodity that exists today were held in much higher esteem and saved for special occasions. Huge capons were perfectly suited to feed a family at Easter or Christmas. Chemical caponising or the neutering of a male chicken has been banned in the UK in for nigh on forty years, but when carried out it produced birds for the table where the weight could be increased to between seven and ten pounds, the meat was moist and tender with any tendencies toward a gamey flavour reduced. Some birds are sold as capons today, but if home bred, these are reared more slowly and given time to attain larger sizes, they are in effect just large chickens.

Cheap cuts were favoured for soups, stews, pies and savoury puddings when long cooking times would tenderise the meat.

Sides of bacon would hang in butchers shops, sliced to order onto a sheet of greaseproof paper, proper bacon without the water.

Heads, feet, ears and tails – everything was used to put a meal on the table. Whatever was put in front of them, children were expected to eat, if not it would reappear at the next mealtime and definitely no pudding if dinner was not eaten.

Sunday roast

Sunday would not have been complete without mothers roast, served with vegetables from the garden and all the trimmings. Whether it was lamb, beef or pork there seems to be a common thread, a generous joint of meat transformed into a lump of charcoal. Caramelised and black on the outside, grey in the middle. Rare cooked meat was rare indeed in the Black Country. But when it was cooked right… Big ribs of beef, fat glistening on the outside, pink in the middle and surrounded by crisp, golden roasties, served with searingly hot mustard and puffed up Yorkshires. Leftover Yorkshire puds were also recycled; sugar, butter and jam transformed them from dinner to dessert. Who doesn't fondly remember roast dinners from childhood, the food, the atmosphere and the family coming together?

Dripping sandwich (bread and scrape, piece of dripping)

This has to be beef or pork dripping. Years ago, well, in my time anyway, this was regarded as something of a delicacy. Today's children and dieticians would roll their eyes in horror waiting for signs of arteries clogging. Dripping is the wondrous substance produced as the Sunday joint roasts in the oven, meat juices and fat drip out into the roasting pan.

A little is harvested for the gravy, but in our house at least, the heavy roasting pan, hot from the oven is juggled as it burns the fingers through the tea towel wrapped around both ends, woefully inadequate to protect from the heat. The juices syphoned off into an old pot mug. Once there, they set.

The fat rises to the top setting into a translucent layer above the important bit, the part that makes dripping special. Hidden beneath this semi-solid white layer is chestnut brown jelly, this is where the flavour hides.

A little of each spread on fresh, thick white bread (none of your pre-sliced, ready wrapped cardboard flavoured convenience bread – real bread mind!) or hot toast liberally seasoned with white pepper and salt. Heaven in a cheap, tasty belly filler.

There was also the infamous licker dip – bread dipped in the hot juices as soon as the meat left the pan

Pork

Cooks were resourceful. Everything bar the squael was used on a pig.

Pigs Trotters (Pigs Feet, Pettitoes)

"Pigs feet, boiling away, delish with some salt on. Sticky fingers, sucking on the bones."

Trotters wax and wane in popularity, with not a great many fans at present and even less in the younger generation, but the old have many fond memories of the cheap, nourishing meals they provided.

Simply put, the name says it all; pigs feet complete with hairs between the toes are a traditional dish in the Black Country. A name not so often used nowadays is pettitoes. Generally, the feet have already been cleaned and the hairs removed when you buy them, any remaining hairs can be singed off if you do not like the idea of eating hairy feet.

Eating pig's feet for the uninitiated can be something of a culture shock. It is not the taste so much as the appearance. The skin will split and curl, lumps of flesh may float away, little bones punctuate the stock and the odd bristle pokes out of an unidentified piece of tissue, all boiling away in a bubbling broth. Delicious with a little salt. When the feet are done, the meat will begin to come away from the bone, there are pieces of skin, meat (not much meat, but there is some), tendon, fat and a surprisingly large number of small bones for a single foot.

Sticky fingers resulted from eating trotters and sucking on the bones. The breakdown of collagen fibres in the trotters results in a glutinous stock that could gum little fingers together while children ate. As the feet breakdown the skin will be meltingly soft (hairy between the toes if not cleaned properly, but no matter), so much so you could suck it through a straw, well a wide one anyway. Any juices left in the pot will set to a jelly that is an ideal flavouring stock.

Not as easy to come by as they once were, but they are about. Ask the butcher or check the markets, after all, pigs have the same number of feet now that they have always had.

Most memories are of boiled trotters, but they also roast well, possibly with maple or honey glaze, or are quite at home in a silky broth of pigs feet soup. Grilling trotters split in half will give you a delicious, chewy skin with some crispy bits, don't put them too close to the heat source at first, give them chance to dry out a little or the skin will burn before the rest is done.

The recipe here is for pigs trotters cooked in a pressure cooker, the onions cook until sweet and tender, fabulous, one of the best parts of the dish.

<u>Pressure cooked pig' feet</u>

2 large trotters, ask the butcher to chop these in half so that they fit in the pressure cooker, or use smaller ones – whatever is to hand.
4 carrots
3 onions
2 potatoes
Seasoning

Peel the carrots, chop into chunks about 1" in size. Peel and thickly slice the onions. Peel the potatoes and chop into chunks around the same size as the carrots. Place these in the bottom of the pressure cooker. More or less of any of the vegetables will work just as well, the sweetness of the carrots and onions works well with the stickiness of the skin.

Place the trotters on top of the vegetables and add enough water to cover. Season well. Peppercorns, bay leaves, cloves, garlic or spices could be added, or just season with good old-fashioned salt and pepper.

Bring up to pressure and boil for around an hour. If the trotters are done, the meat and skin will be soft and tender, beginning to come away from the bones.

Remove from the cooking liquor and serve.

Pigs head

"Mom used to boil the pig's head in a big black pot, but the ears used to keep lifting the lid off. Once they sent the pig's head with the eyes still in. Mom couldn't get it out, so she put the lot in the pot... The lid kept coming up and the eye peepin' out........so funny." Catherine Flavell

Cooking a whole pigs head is not as easy as people may think. This is not from an aesthetic point of view, but to a person who does not feel comfortable eating anything with eyes on it being confronted by an entire head is somewhat disturbing. Without a doubt, there is good meat in there, but this piece of meat has a face on it. It is also a big, serious hunk of meat, needing a large pan, but it does make an impressive centrepiece on the table, with or without an apple in its mouth.

If a pan is to hand of suitable size for an entire head, boil until the meat is tender enough to easily remove the bones. Use stuffing to reform the head, season the skin, transfer to a medium oven and roast as any other pork joint, basting occasionally. Serve with the usual accompaniments to pork.

Brawn

"If you touched the teeth when you were pulling the meat away – urgh! The tongue was ok though, once the skin was off."

What may the reader ask is brawn? Well, this is chopped pork meat set in a jelly of its own making, produced as the bones, cartilage, skin and other tissues boil down into a gelatinous mass which sets as it cools, the whole thing flavoured with herbs and possibly other additions. The "and other" is what can change the character of the dish. Sage works well with pork and is an ideal flavouring. Parsley is a common additive lending a fresh taste and colour. Lemon will lift the dish. Masses of pepper is a traditional slant, but anything goes, as it would have done back in the days when austerity was the driving force.

You could go a step further with the pig's feet mentioned in the above recipe and use them to produce brawn. Reserve the liquid the feet were cooked in, remove the meat from the trotters and chop finely, add this to a container with a few pieces of the cooked carrot, pour the cooking liquid over and chill until set.

Brawn is generally made using a mix of pigs head and trotters or pigs head alone, but whatever type of head is to hand may be substituted. It is usual to remove the eyes and brain before cooking. The dish has a mild flavour and soft texture, the addition of thinly sliced carrot adds a pleasant sweetness and, given that people "eat with their eyes," the orange colour can make the finished dish more appetising. It could almost be described as meat jelly, small pieces of cooked pigs head congealed in a seasoned gelatinous gloop. Very tasty.

Speaking of added interest, here is another factoid. In North America, brawn goes by the slightly disconcerting name of headcheese.

It is possible to find a butcher who cooks and sells their own brawn, they are rare now, but unlike the unicorn, some do exist. Whether you buy it or cook it, the dish is usually eaten cold, sliced on sandwiches or chunked for eating as it comes.

There are many variations of the recipe. One question is to brine or not to brine. It is debatable which gives the best flavour and there are considerable variations on how long the head should sit in the brine, some say hours, others a day and some up to two weeks. The brine should act as a preservative, but will also impart a ham like quality.

<u>Brine</u>

1 lb salt – use pure salt if possible, not one with anti-caking ingredients
6 pints water
Seasoning or spices to taste

<u>Brawn</u>
3 pig's trotters
1 pigs head
3 onions
3 carrots
Seasoning

Optional: 2 leeks
3 celery stalks
A few sage leaves
Parsley

Spices are optional, but if used the flavour will seep into every pore and give the finished brawn more depth. Pickling spice, peppercorns, bay or coriander could also be included, whatever floats your boat and flavours your pig.

A large pan is a necessity for this, big enough to fit in a pig's head, and trotters, if using. Ask the butcher to cut the head in half and remove the brain. Make up the brine by adding the salt to the water, which may need heating in order for the salt to dissolve fully. Cool. Test the brine to see if the concentration is strong enough by dropping in a raw potato. If this sinks the brine is too weak, the potato should bob up and down near the surface if the concentration is right.

Remove the ears from the head and retain these, remove any hairs. The modernists can use a blowtorch for this job, traditionalists may prefer to singe off the hairs using a lighted candle. Place the head in the brine and leave for 24 hours. You may wish to quarter the head so it better fits the pan.

Next, prepare the brawn. Place the head in a pan of cold water; add the ears and trotters. Peel and thickly slice the onions and carrots, add these to the pan. The leeks and celery may be added at this point if they are being used. Season and add any spices.

Bring to the boil, skim any scum from the surface and boil for about three hours, making sure it does not boil dry. Burnt pig does not have the best flavour!

Remove the head from the boiling liquor and unless the fingers are made of asbestos, allow the head to cool enough to handle comfortably, before picking off all the available meat. Do not throw away the liquid. Anything that looks edible can be salvaged, the cheek meat is good, so is the meat around the eye sockets and believe it or not the snout. There is more useable meat at the back of the head. Once the head has been cleaned of every scrap, chop the meat into smallish chunks of around 1cm.

More scum may have settled on top of the liquid, remove this, the stock should be as clear as possible for the brawn, sieving or straining through muslin helps here. Adding a beaten egg white collects more of the impurities. Stir this into the cooling stock (not cold), it will poach in the liquid and float to the surface catching these impurities that can then be removed along with the egg white as it is scooped out of the stock.

Adjust the seasoning. Do not add too much salt – this cannot be taken out, do not be shy with the pepper. Put the meat into a mould; use a decorative one or even a jelly mould. Press well in, some of the onion and carrot can be added. Thinly sliced carrot adds a good note of colour, as does fresh parsley. Pour in enough stock to fill the mould and refrigerate until set, ideally overnight.

Lining the mould with Clingfilm before filling will make the brawn easier to turn out, alternatively dip the mould into hot water for a few seconds to loosen. Turn out onto a plate and enjoy.

Chawl (Pigs cheeks)

"Mom used to boil a pig's head till the bones dropped out, then mince the meat and press it in a basin. Delish" Catherine Flavell

This term is seldom used now, chawl is made in the same way as brawn, but only the cheeks or jowls of the pig are used, giving a meatier result. The head was cleaned and brined, then boiled until the meat fell off the bones. This was cooled and the cheek meat finely chopped and seasoned. Pepper is a good friend of pork, plenty was added with enough salt to bring out the flavour.

The cut up meat would then be placed into a basin, pot or mould and a little of the cooking liquor added, the gelatine from the pork sets the liquid into a jelly. A plate smaller in diameter than the mould would be placed on top of the meat and weighted down with something heavy, a tin can or two could be used for this if there are no weights. This will produce a pressed meat for slicing, similar to brawn and perfect for sandwiches.

Pigs Cheek

There is more to pigs cheeks than brawn, these are seriously good in their own right, just how good is another well-kept secret. The meat is located below the eye, in the hollow of the cheek. Still a little-known cut, this used to be incredibly cheap but as word is spreading, the price is increasing. They can also be difficult to get hold of, occasionally they can be found on sale, but more than likely these will need to be ordered. Meltingly tender, moist and tasty, cheek still requires a long, slow cook to be enjoyed at its best, boiling or braising works well.

Years ago they would be soaked in a brine of salt, sugar and water for several days, before being poached in fresh water and served, then eaten either hot or cold. Bath chaps were cooked pigs cheeks covered in breadcrumbs then deep-fried.

Brine

4oz sugar
12oz salt – use pure salt, not one with anti-caking ingredients
2 pints water
1 bay leaf

Put all the ingredients for the brine into a pan and heat gently until the sugar and salt have dissolved. Allow the brine to cool and soak the pork cheeks in the brine for several hours or longer.

Braised pigs cheeks are suitable for serving as a dinner, bearing in mind the long cooking time, possibly better to save them for the weekend. Many recipes recommend braising in red wine to help tenderise the meat. Allow a couple of cheeks per person.

4 pigs cheeks
1 onion
1 carrot
1 clove of garlic

½ pint red wine
Sprig of thyme
½ pint stock
Lard to fry
Knob of butter

Preheat the oven to 160°C. Peel and finely slice the onion, peel and chop the carrot, peel and chop the garlic. Fry these gently until they start to soften, be careful not to let the garlic burn or it will be bitter. Transfer to an ovenproof dish. Fry the pig's cheeks on each side until sealed and browned. Add the thyme and the wine, increase the heat and boil until the wine has reduced by around half before transferring the cheeks and reduction to the ovenproof dish. Add the stock and cook in the oven for three hours, when the meat should be tender.

Use the cooking liquid to make a gravy, decant from the cheeks into a pan, add a knob of butter and heat to reduce. The sauce should thicken. If it remains too thin, slake a little cornflour and use this to thicken the sauce.

Serve with mashed potatoes, carrots, peas and, of course, apple sauce.

Pigs Ears

You cannot make a silk purse out of a sow's ear, but you can make a tasty meal. Still popular in cuisine around the world, pigs ears are included in soul food menu's across the States, served roast with soy in China, the name of the dish ceng ceng cui translates as layers of crunch, they are roast as part of tapas in Spain or popular as a dog treat in the UK. Of course, it was not always like that, all the pig was eaten and the ears could be a tasty snack, but first they were subject to boiling, frying or a combination of both.

Marjorie Cashmore in her book A Feast of Memories: Black Country Food and Life at the Turn of the Century, talks of soaking the ears for hours before boiling them with trotters, later adding vinegar and salt to a little of the water and allowing this to set. The ears were then sliced, battered and fried before serving with mustard, butter and more vinegar.

Should you wish to try these, two recipes are given below.

4 pig's ears
Salt
Oil to fry

Trim the ears and singe off any remaining hairs. Cut out the lumpy, ridged inner section, leaving the flatter, lower flap. Boil these for ages, hours, in fact, about five hours should do it until these little flaps of pig are tender. Take them out of the water and cool the ears. Dry these off before slicing into thin strips, season well and serve with vinegar and mustard.

Alternatively, cook as above, cut into thin strips, coat in flour and flash fry in lard or dripping until the colour of pork scratchings and serve in the same way as scratchings, accompanied by a good pint of beer.

Pigs Snouts

Nose to tail eating was practised in the Black Country long before it became fashionable, but there is something about the sight of those little round snouts and the nostrils that makes me shudder. Usually, the snout is cooked while still attached to the pig's head, which is fine, but once removed to be dried and packaged in bags for dog treats, they just look so wrong. All those poor pigs missing a snout!

For human consumption, there is a little more attached than the very tip of the snout, and to be fair, there is meat and fat in abundance. The snout is taken from where it joins the face and can weigh up to a pound, definitely enough to warrant cooking for a meal.

These can be substituted for the hocks in a ham hock and split pea soup making a very tasty snout soup. Once the snout has simmered, take it out of the stock and add back some bits to the broth. You can also pan fry pieces of the snout as with the ears, there will be the soft, gelatinous layer topped with crispy, tasty skin. Those snouts are sounding a whole lot better now.

Pigs Tail

This curly appendage was not wasted. Not much on a tail, you may think, but it is after all, still pork. Think how good the skin tastes from trotters and hocks after boiling, unctuous, soft, melting and sticky. There is everything there, remember how adding bone to soups and stocks improves the flavour, well it's all here in the tail, porky flavoured meat, more of this than you would expect and bones to suck on after you've guzzled all the meat. The old folk would happily suck every last vestige of flavour out of the bones of tails and trotters before discarding them with a clatter onto the plate and sit back replete and satisfied, a porky glow radiating from the stomach out. Oh and one more thing – ask for longer tails.

The meat can be tough if not prepared in the right way, as with most bits of the pig, long slow cooking works best, such as braising. To try to tempt the modern palate to try this old-fashioned part of the pig, the recipe is modern Asian style, if you want tradition, ditch the marinade and braise with carrots and onions.

<u>Braised pork tails</u>

Pigs tails, try to get longer ones

<u>Marinade</u>

1 clove garlic
Half bottle of soy sauce
1 red chilli, seeds removed and chopped
1 tablespoon honey
1 tablespoon demerara or soft brown sugar
1 lime – juice and peel

1 onion, peeled and sliced
½" root ginger, peeled and thinly sliced

Braising vegetables
1 onion sliced
1 carrot chopped
½ pint water.

Put the tails into an ovenproof dish. Peel the garlic, sprinkle a little salt on the chopping board and place the garlic on top. Put the flat side of a knife on top of the clove of garlic and wallop it with the heel of the hand to crush the garlic and add this to the dish along with the rest of the marinade ingredients. Give this a good squidge with the hands to make sure the tails are coated in the mix. Cover with foil and store in the fridge for a couple of hours, or overnight if there is time.

Preheat the oven to 170°C, 340°F, Gas Mk 3. Place the onions and carrots under the tails. Add the water, put a lid on the dish and cook for 4 hours until sticky and very tender. Check the dish has not boiled dry every half an hour or so and top up with water or stock as necessary.

Pork hock and split peas

Nourishing, tasty, simple. Granny's ham hock and split pea soup, nothing else needs saying – just enjoy. In a way, this is just another variation of grey peas and bacon. Ham hocks are readily available in butchers shops, use a ham or gammon hock rather than pork, the flavour will be better. There are a little further up the leg than trotters, with the same sticky, gelatinous depth of flavour associated with the meltdown of skin, bone and sinew into stock. Cured pork has a tendency to be salty, so if salt intake is an issue soak the hock overnight and rinse well before using. If not cook as is; the result may be a little salty for some tastes, but if the preference is for well-seasoned food that should be fine. Hocks do vary in salt content; if in doubt ask the butcher when you buy. If hocks are difficult to source, at a push, bacon could be substituted.

Then, there are the peas. Not the average Birds Eye frozen variety, but something with more staying power - split peas. If green ones aren't available, go for the yellow variety, they might need soaking before use, check the pack as this is not always a requirement. Soaked or not, cook them well until they begin to break down and thicken the soup.

Takes a bit of forward planning this one, not fast food by any means.

1 ham hock
3 onions
2 carrots
1 stick of celery
1 lb split peas, green or yellow
Bay leaf
Sprig of thyme

Soak the peas in water and set aside while you make the ham stock. This could be done in a pressure cooker to speed things up a little. Put the hock into a large pan with a peeled onion sliced into quarters, roughly chop a carrot and the celery and throw these into the pan with the thyme. Do not season at this stage, as you will not know how salty the hock is. Add just enough water to cover and bring to the boil. Skim off any scum rising to the surface. Simmer until the meat is tender, this should take around three hours. Turn off the heat and let this cool in the pan. Remove the hock from the cooking liquid, do not throw this away, you will need it later, but remove the vegetables from the liquor; these are done with and can be discarded.

Peel and chop the remaining two onions, slice and chop the carrot. Fry these together in a large pan until the onion is soft and beginning to caramelise. Strain the peas and add them to the onion and carrot in the pan. Mix well to coat in the lard and warm through, deglaze the pan with some of the ham stock then add around a litre of stock. Turn up the heat to bring the soup to the boil then simmer for at least an hour by when the peas should be starting to break down and thicken the soup. Keep an eye on the soup to make sure it does not catch or boil dry, add more stock as necessary.

Remove all the meat from the ham bone and roughly chop this, add it to the soup, adjust the seasoning as necessary and serve.

Grey Peas and Bacon (Gray paes and baercun)

As the recipes unfold throughout the book, a bit of a theme may appear to develop, cooking pots and pet shops. It is a wonder that good nutritious pulses and grains, such as grey peas, groats and pin head oatmeal have been relegated to the pet shops while trendy chefs in upmarket restaurants boasting Michelin stars claim to have discovered the delights of offal. Black Country folk could have taught them a thing or two about offal generations ago! There is a bonus with grey peas; these can be found in fishing shops too.

Grey peas and bacon have been served up in the Black Country for a very long time; the dish is something of a variation on pease pudding, tasty and nutritious with the peas providing a rich source of protein and fibre.

These hard, dried peas are also known as maple peas, pigeon peas or carlins. Tiny, round cannon balls that need to be soaked before cooking. Pigeon peas give a clue to where you can buy these and pet shops are one source, but some butchers, greengrocers or health food shops may also stock them.

Northerners may try to claim "black peas" as their own, they too traditionally serve them on bonfire night, but – and it's a big but – they serve theirs slathered in vinegar. In the Black Country, they are prepared as a protein-rich thick soup or cooked down further into a stew. Grey pea and bacon soup was given away by innkeepers in the Black Country to their customers on Fastens E'en, more commonly known as Shrove Tuesday now, or home fare on Ash Wednesday.

There are many recipes for this dish, but all very similar in their ingredients, some also include pearl barley but we never have. Below is my version of Black Country Gray Paes and Baercun.

8oz grey peas (before soaking)
4oz bacon bits
1 tsp bicarbonate of soda
Seasoning.

Put the grey peas in a large bowl, they will swell considerably so allow plenty of room in the bowl. Add a teaspoon of bicarbonate of soda and fill the bowl ¾ full with cold water. Leave overnight.

Rinse well and transfer the peas to a large pan, they should not swell further if they were soaked overnight. Add the bacon. Some people prefer to fry the bacon beforehand but this can be added straight from the pack, smoked or unsmoked, back or streaky, just use what you have. Go easy on the seasoning at this point, as bacon can be salty, better to adjust at the end. Add sufficient water to cover and top up as necessary during cooking, do not allow the peas to boil dry. Either bring to the boil on the stovetop or in a pressure cooker or slow cooker, it will work by any method. If you are cooking on the stove top watch it doesn't catch and cook until the peas are tender, this can take at least a couple of hours. Cook down until the cooking liquor forms its own sauce and the peas are starting to break down a little and very soft. Adjust the seasoning to taste.

You could fry an onion until caramelised and add that when you put the bacon in, some people add stock instead of water to cook the peas or add an Oxo cube to the water.
Serve with crusty bread.

Brummie Bacon Cakes (Brummie Breakfast Cakes)

The jury is out as to whether or not these should be included in a collection of Black Country recipes as Birmingham is not, and strictly never has been part of the Black Country. But so many people have described these savoury scones as seriously good that it would be criminal to allow the recipe to vanish, so as a service to the Midlands, here it is.

4 rashers of streaky bacon – diced
4oz grated mature cheddar
8oz self-raising flour
¼ pint milk
2oz butter
Pinch salt
Pepper
1 tablespoon tomato sauce (optional)
1 tablespoon Worcester sauce (optional)

Fry the bacon. Rub the butter into the flour until it resembles fine breadcrumbs. Stir through two-thirds of the cheese and season well. Add the bacon, the tomato and Worcester sauces then just enough milk to make a soft dough. Roll to about ½" thick and cut out eight rounds. Alternatively, form into one large round and cut 8 wedges. Brush with milk and sprinkle over the remaining cheese and bake in a hot oven (180-200oC, 400oF, Gas Mk 6) until well risen and golden, around 20-30 minutes.

Serve as part of a breakfast, with beans and egg, split and butter them or simply serve with a fried egg.

This is not a new food item, variations of this recipe have surfaced repeatedly, with anecdotal evidence going back as far as the 1860's of flat baked cakes and in September 1945, the Tamworth Herald published an extract from the Ministry of Food facts number 8 – Making the Most of Bacon, and there was recipe for Bacon Cakes.

Beef

As with pigs, there is very little on a cow that cannot be eaten, recipes exist for heads, udders, tails and every bit in between, inside and out.

In the Black Country, a great tradition exists for pig and ox roasts. The Black Country Bugle has carried a number of informative articles about this, including those about Harry Johnson, which make for interesting reading.

A cow is a fair sized animal to roast in front of an open fire, the Hereford Bull cooked at the Jubilee Celebrations in the grounds of Dudley Castle on 11th May 1935 weighed in at 12cwt live. Harry Johnson, the Black Country's own self-styled "Worlds Champion Ox Roaster" oversaw the four hour long roasting by a fire stoked with a ton of coal, the turning of the beast all done by hand on a solidly built spit with a pole akin to a telegraph pole to stand the weight.

The heat from the fire teased out the fats and juices as the ox roast, the smell must have got the juices flowing in the large crowd too. There was a call for coppers (small change, pennies and ha'pennies) so the children could have a piece of dip. The roaring trade in this kept the helpers busy until the meat was cooked.

At 6 pm, Mayor, Alderman W.C. Williams, carved the first slice. Another tradition at ox roasts was the auction of the first sandwich and this day was no different. The Earl of Dudley paid the princely sum of £5, before giving back the sandwich to be sold again.

Harry's career as an ox roaster spanned many a function between the 1920's and when he finally put down the spit on 10th September

1966 at the Bilston Conservative Association Barbecue, but things did not go well on Harry's swansong. Sturdy though it was, the spit was not sturdy enough, buckling under the weight, the beast could not be turned. Twenty men valiantly attempted to straighten it but failed.

"Chaos at the Barbeque" read the headlines, the buckling of the spit was not the only problem that day. Inconsiderate parking slowed the traffic, queues reached from Sedgley Bull Ring back to Wombourne, with many people not even making it into the venue. Of those who did, one wonders, did they notice the late change to the menu from Roast Beef to fried? Slabs of beef were fried in skillets and served up to the crowd.

Cow heels

Another nutritious, sticky meat, this is the chunky cartilage forming the heel of the joint, often boiled until it formed a thick, gloopy, gelatinous mixture. Again, the dish has fallen out of fashion over the years in the UK but still popular elsewhere. Recipes included such delights as cow heel pie, cowheel soup, cow heel with green sauce or simple boiling and serving in a napkin with butter and mustard.

I confess to never having cooked these, nor even seen them for sale in a butcher's shop.

A typical way of cooking would be to obtain the cow heels, boil until these are tender. Then chop these into fair size chunks before dipping first into egg, then breadcrumbs and fry until golden. Present this with caramelised onions. The saltiness of bacon and fat pork sausages work well when served alongside cow heel.

The liquid in which the cow heels were cooked can be used to form the base for a soup, similar to that obtained when cooking pig's feet.

Ox Cheek (beef cheek)

The cheek muscle of the cow is another cheap cut of meat used to eke out the weekly housekeeping, but these days this can be difficult to find. Frugal housewives managed to make a dual-purpose dish that could serve two meals. The meat itself is both lean and dense, but it can be tough so long slow cooking to help tenderise the meat is a must and care should be taken to prevent it from drying out. Cheek is ideally suited to soups or casseroles, or a dish that combines both, where the meat is cooked in broth. The meat is then removed from the liquor and served with vegetables and the broth reheated to provide another meal on another day. Cooking in a slow cooker is ideal for this cut, but whichever method you use, trim the meat well, remove any excess fat and the silvery membrane which may be gristly, leaving pure beef cheek meat, cook it long, cook it slow and enjoy.

Despite the long cooking time, cheek is worth a try, old recipes recommended soaking for several hours before cooking. You could soak in a marinade to add extra flavour, cheeks take up the flavour of the braising liquid well and many popular recipes involve braising in red wine. Careful trimming and slow cooking should be adequate to produce a warm, comforting dish of tender beef.

Ox cheek
1 pint good beef stock
2 onions, peeled and sliced
1 leek, sliced
1 clove garlic, peeled and chopped
Stick of celery, diced
2 carrots, peeled and sliced
1 tablespoon of tomato puree
Sprig of thyme
1 tablespoon plain flour, seasoned with salt and pepper

Trim anything you would not want to eat off the cheek, including any excess fat and all the tough, silvery membranes that may be gristly on eating. You could marinate the beef overnight in red wine, which will also help to tenderise it.

Slice the beef into strips and coat with the seasoned flour, fry until browned then transfer to a casserole dish or slow cooker. Add the onions, leeks, garlic and celery to the fat and fry gently until they begin to soften, transfer these to the casserole dish. Add the sliced carrots, tomato puree, thyme and stock. Put a lid on the casserole dish and place in a preheated oven at 150°C for about four hours until the meat is meltingly tender. Stir in a glass of port and if you like a sweeter taste a tablespoon of redcurrant jelly, return to the oven for half an hour. Serve on a bed of mashed potato.

Ox cheek was also popular during the war years, no meat would have been wasted and stews were an excellent method of making what little there was go further. The following recipe is reproduced courtesy of the Black Country Bugle newspaper, published weekly promoting the history of the region.

Wartime Food Facts Recipe – Reproduced by kind permission of the Black Country Bugle.

Stewed Ox Cheek (serves 4 - 6)

1 ox cheek
2 or 3 carrots
A bunch of herbs
1oz flour
1 parsnip
1 small turnip
1oz margarine
Salt and pepper

"Wash the cheek well in warm water, then put in a saucepan, cover with cold water, bring to the boil and skim thoroughly. Add the vegetables, sliced, and the herbs and seasoning. Stew very slowly, keeping just enough liquid in the pan to cover, for 3 to 4 hours, or until the bones come away from the cheek easily.

Melt the margarine in a pan, mix in the flour smoothly, cook for 2 or 3 minutes, then slowly add one pint of the liquid from the pan and bring to the boil, stirring all the time. Season if necessary.

Remove the bones from the meat, pour the sauce over and simmer together for 10 minutes before serving."

Calves Head

Popular years ago, not so much now, there are still many people who remember cooking and enjoying both pigs and sheep's head, though not quite so many calves' heads. They are still available to buy, but an unusual choice for the home cook, a recipe is included below should people wish to try. There are many other methods of preparing a calf's head for the table, they can be roast, stewed, hashed, there is no need to stop at boiling.

Boiled Calf's Head

Place the calf's head in a large pan and boil for ten minutes, remove and scrape off the hair. As the head cools this may become more difficult to remove, place it back in the boiling water for a few minutes before carrying on. When all the hair has been removed, cut off the ears, and then remove the eyes, tongue and brain. Soak the brain in cold water overnight.

Put the head and the tongue into a large pan, cover with cold water and add 2 sliced onions, 2 sliced carrots, 1 sliced stick of celery, a sprig of thyme and a bay leaf. Bring to the boil, then turn the heat down and simmer for 2 hours, skim off any scum. Strain and put the head and tongue back in the cold water, discard the vegetables. Season the head and boil for another hour or two, again remove any scum that appears. Add more carrots, celery, potatoes and a clove-studded onion to the water and more herbs. Boil for a further hour until the vegetables are tender.

Remove some of the cooking liquid to a small pan and add the brain to this, simmer for half an hour until the brain is set. When the meat in the calves head is tender, take the pan off the heat. Remove the tongue and flay this, cut into slices. Hard boil 3 eggs peel and quarter these. Remove the vegetables from the cooking water to a plate, lay the head on top of these, arrange the tongue and brain around the head, decorate this with the egg.

Pies and Puddings

Pudding and pies, steak and kidney or meat and potato were popular mid-week meal choices. Gravy thick and rich, full of flavour, meltingly soft meat packed into a crisp, golden pastry case. What could be better? Pudding! Steak and Kidney pudding, the kidney imparts a wonderful richness to the gravy and the energy packed into a soft, suet crust could sustain a whole day of hard work. Traditional food at its best.

<u>Slow Cooker Steak and kidney pudding</u>

Suet pastry may sound unappetising, a thick, stodgy mix of grated beef fat, flour and a little salt, boiled or steamed for hours, but something magical happens during the cooking process, it matters little whether the filling is sweet or savoury. The heavy, lumpen mass transforms into a golden moreish fluffy coating hugging the hidden contents and the taste? Sublime and the smell as it cooks will be heavenly (unless the cooking takes place in a slow cooker when the smell does not seem to match the taste).

The high fat content of the pastry means it is not the most fashionable of dishes but brings back some wonderful memories of sitting down to dinner in a bitter winter. If ever there was a food designed to fend off an arctic blast, it was this one.

A little more time consuming to put together and a while in the cooking but the result is worth the extra effort. At least ready grated suet is available in its bright blue and red box, this has simplified the task of making the pastry, though you can if you like grate or chop finely the hard beef fat from around the kidneys of the beast.

Suet pastry

8oz self-raising flour
4oz suet
Pinch salt
Cold water to bind

Filling

1 lb steak
3 pig's kidneys
Salt
Pepper
2 onions
Mixed herbs (optional)
¾ pint Stock
1 tablespoon of Worcester sauce
2 tablespoons of flour
Knob of lard

Put the slow cooker on, with about 2" water in the bottom. Make the pastry by putting the flour, suet and salt in a bowl. Add enough water so that you can bring it together to form a soft dough.

Keep around a third of the pastry back for the lid, roll the rest to about 1/3" thick, and use this to line a greased two-pint pudding basin. Make sure there are no splits in the pastry for the gravy to leak through.

Next, make the filling. The basis of the dish is steak and kidney, but the steak need not be an expensive cut; anything that lends itself to long slow cooking will do just fine. You can use braising steak, stewing steak, flank, or skirt. Lambs kidneys work well; you could use pigs or ox, but whichever one you use, trim the kidney removing the tough interior part then dice the softer exterior. Cut the steak into similar size pieces. Season the flour and coat the meat in the flour.

Chop the onion while the lard heats in a casserole dish or saucepan. Fry the onion gently until it starts to soften then add the meat and continue to fry until the meat is lightly browned. Transfer the meat and onions to the suet crust lined bowl. Deglaze the frying pan by adding any leftover seasoned flour to the frying pan with the Worcester sauce, mixed herbs if these are being used and the stock, stir to mix. Cook for a few minutes while it thickens then pour over the steak and kidney; fill the bowl to about 1" from the top. Keep the rest of the gravy to serve with the pudding later. Roll out the rest of the pastry, dampen the edges and place the lid on top, press down to seal.

Butter a sheet of foil or greaseproof paper large enough to cover the top of the pudding and overlap the sides. Fold a pleat into this to allow for expansion and place it buttered side down on the pudding. Tie this in place with string; create a handle with the string to make it easier to lift the pudding out later and place this in the slow cooker. Cook on high for between 5 and 6 hours or steam on the stovetop for 2 ½ hours until cooked through. Do not allow the pan to boil dry, top up with boiling water as necessary. Alternatively, you could cook in a bain-marie in the oven.

Turn out and serve with the extra gravy.

Meat and potato pie

Instead of suet crust, this has a shortcrust pastry lid, lovely with gravy and a firm favourite when Nan used to produce it hot from the oven.

Filling
2lb braising steak
2lb potatoes
2 onions
Oxo cube
1 tablespoon flour

Pastry
4oz lard
8oz plain flour
Pinch of salt
Milk to glaze

Cut the steak into cubes and peel and slice the onions, season a tablespoon of flour and coat the meat in this. Fry the onions and the meat until the onions are beginning to soften and the meat is browned. Dissolve the Oxo cube in a pint of water. Transfer meat, onions and Oxo to a pan, bring to the boil then simmer for around 2 hours until tender. You could use a pressure cooker for this stage to speed things up.

Then make the pastry. Add a pinch of salt to the flour. Cut the fat into small pieces in the flour, and then use the fingertips to rub until the pastry looks like breadcrumbs. Add enough cold water to mix to a firm dough. Knead slightly until the pastry comes together into a ball but do not overwork or the pastry will be hard. Chill for half an hour.

While the pastry is chilling, boil the potatoes, not so long as they are too soft. Drain and cut into chunks.

Preheat the oven to 200°C, transfer the meat to an ovenproof dish and add the potatoes. If the gravy is too thin, thicken this up either with gravy granules or mix a dessertspoon of flour with a little water in a cup and add to the pan, bring to the boil, stirring until thickened and add enough to the meat in the dish to cover the meat and potatoes. Roll the pastry out to about ¼" thick, large enough to make a lid for the dish. Dampen the rim of the dish and put on the lid, press the edges down to seal the pie. Poke a small hole in the centre of the top to let the steam out and brush the top with milk. Bake for 45 minutes to an hour until the top is golden. Serve hot with vegetables and the extra gravy.

Potato topped pies

Although there are others, the two obvious contenders are cottage pie and shepherd's pie. Evidence for cottage pies predates the shepherd's pie by nigh on a hundred years. It is generally accepted that a cottage pie is made with beef and shepherd's pie, lamb. The term shepherd's pie links to obvious origins, but cottage pie, how does this link to beef? Cottage pie would have been a term for any pie filled with chopped or minced meat and topped with potatoes. The term came about as potatoes became cheap food for the masses. The people would live in cottages and as the food became more commonly eaten, so the name cottage pie came into usage. In a cottage pie, the potatoes were sliced, not mashed, and arranged over the top like the tiles on the roof of a cottage. The dish itself could be lined with potato forming a "coffin" for the meat. Both versions used leftover meat and vegetables to eke out rations and feed the hungry.

Cottage Pie

A gravy rich mixture of meat and potato with a crispy top. Slips down with hardly the need to chew and costs virtually nothing as it uses up the leftovers from Sunday lunch. Perfection in a pie dish. Where the potato touches the edges of the pie dish, it will weld a crust of burnt potato that is well worth the effort to scrape off and eat when there is no one else looking. There was always a fight for this.

Cooked beef – doesn't matter which cut, left over from Sunday lunch
Onion
Mashed potato
Gravy
Leftover vegetables

Mince the beef left over from a roasting joint and together with an onion. If there were any roast potatoes or parsnips, you could mince these too. Alternatively, you could grate or thinly slice an onion. Fry this first to caramelise it, the flavour will be sweeter. Place meat and onion into an ovenproof dish and pour over any leftover gravy. A cottage pie is not complete without gravy. If there is not enough left make extra, worst case scenario use instant but try to avoid this at all costs if you can. If there was any dripping left over use this to gently fry the onion, add a dessertspoonful of flour and fry until the flour is cooked. Gradually add half a pint of water, if you had to cook extra potatoes or vegetables for the pie, use the water from these to give extra flavour. Add a splash of gravy browning for colour and use this to moisten the meat in the dish. Mix in any leftover vegetables and top with the mashed potato. Place in a moderate oven until heated through and the top has browned. Serve with extra vegetables if you need it to go further.

Shepherd's Pie
Prepared as above, but the leftover meat would have been lamb or mutton, not beef.

Groaty pudding (grorty pudding, grutty, groaty dick, even dirty dick)

Fewer and fewer people have heard of groats now, even less cooked with them, yet when cooked correctly they are tasty, cheap and highly nutritious. Any variety of grains can be included under the heading of groats, including oat, barley, rye or wheat, the latter being otherwise known as bulgur wheat. These should have been subject to relatively little processing, possibly hulling and crushing. Oats offering the highest level of nutrition of all these and are the ones generally used in the Black Country to cook a groaty pudding. Shown left are groats as bought from the pet shop.

These can be sliced, steel cut and steamed into oatmeal, which means they will cook more quickly than whole grains, but this does not necessarily make for a better groaty pudding. Try to find whole grains if you can, where only the husk has been removed. These work better if you are to avoid cooking up a tasty batch of beefy porridge.

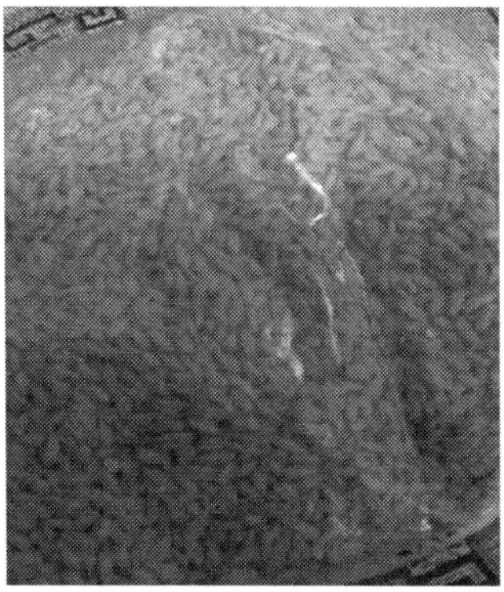

Not often seen in supermarkets, you may find groats in butchers shops that prepare regional dishes or in health food shops, but the most common outlet by far is pet shops, where they are easy to source and cheap to buy.

So, now you know what a groat is, but what is groaty pudding? Traditionally served on bonfire night in the Black Country along with potatoes baked in the embers of the fire, a warming stew that along with groats contains stewing meat, onions, leeks and seasonings.

In order to be tender and palatable, the groats will need long, slow cooking to release all their goodness.

Having trawled the internet for several hours the only concrete conclusion was that there was no definitive recipe for groaty pudding. I remember it as being thick; belly filling, rib stickingly good old-fashioned comfort food. The grains have the same sweetness as pearl barley.

So, do you soak or don't you soak? It really doesn't seem to matter. Do you fry the meat or don't you fry the meat first. You choose. Onions? Possibly. Leeks? Maybe. How many? You decide.

Traditional Black Country fare without question, but the recipe remains elusive. Groaty pudding contains groats, onion, leeks (maybe), stock (if you desire – water if you don't), salt, pepper, carrots (possibly), beef (skirt, stewing steak, sirloin– again you decide).

The groats need to soak, to swell and soften before cooking.

"After an impulse buy of a bag of groats from the pet shop, we picked up some stewing steak to go with them on the way home; we hadn't had groaty pudding for years. The groats went into a bowl to soak at around 6 pm, by 7 pm they filled they vessel, by 8 pm they threatened to take over the kitchen. Safe to say you don't need half a bag full if you're only feeding three."

Looks can be deceiving, don't believe the photo, groaty pudding tastes better than it looks, but it does need plenty of seasoning, salt and pepper, don't skimp on the stock either.

Slow cooker or stove top, it doesn't matter really, the one above was left overnight in a slow cooker, with the smell keeping the dogs who were also in the kitchen, awake till the morning.

1lb stewing steak, cut into cubes
2 cups of groats (about half a pound, possibly less)
1 onion
Stock or 2 Oxo cubes, try to use good quality beef stock, don't skimp on this
2 leeks

Soak the groats for at least a couple of hours, preferably overnight, these will swell considerably. Rinse under cold water. If using a slow cooker at this point the onions and leeks can be sliced, cut the steak into smallish cubes and chuck it all into the pot with the soaked groats and a couple of pints of stock. Season. Put the lid on and leave it to mellow. Several hours or overnight should see it right. Stir occasionally as the groats may still swell and they may stick if this is the case.

If it looks too thin, thicken up the gravy with a little slaked cornflour, adjust the seasoning and serve with crusty bread and butter.

If cooking on the stovetop or in the oven, again soak the groats overnight, then rinse. Fry the onions gently to caramelise, then add the leeks and fry till soft. Transfer to a large pan. Season the steak and fry until lightly browned, transfer this to the pan. Carrots could be added for extra flavour. Add the stock, around two pints, but keep an eye on it while cooking; this may need to topping up. Stir in the groats and season. Pop it in a medium over for around three hours or simmer on the stove top, stirring occasionally as the groats have a tendency to cling together, safety in numbers and all that, then they stick and the last thing you want in burnt groats in your pudding.

When the groats are tender, it's done. Simple.

Tweak the seasoning, add a bit of gravy browning if you like it darker, boil it down for thicker gravy and serve with crusty bread.

Braised beef with onions

High on taste, but low on effort, here again long slow cooking results in meltingly tender meat. Braising steak might be sold as that or shin of beef, but any of the cheaper cuts suited to long slow cooking would be fine.

Braising steaks or shin. 1 per person or you could slice these into chunks
3 onions, peeled and thinly sliced
1 tablespoon flour
1 pint good beef stock
2 tablespoons Worcester sauce
½ tsp dried thyme
Salt and pepper
1 tsp cornflour

Pre-heat the oven to 170°C, 325°F, Gas Mk 3. Trim any fatty or gristly bits off the steaks, then season them, coat with the flour, pat off the excess and fry gently to brown these. Transfer the steak to a heatproof casserole dish and fry the onion until soft and beginning to caramelise. A handful of thinly sliced mushrooms could be added and fried with the onions then transfer these to the casserole dish. Add the stock, Worcester sauce and thyme to the steak and onions. Put a lid on the dish and transfer to the oven for two hours, until the steak is falling apart.

Slake the cornflour with a tablespoon of cold water, then stir this into the gravy, put the casserole back in the oven or place it on the hob to boil up and thicken the gravy. Adjust the seasoning. Serve with potatoes and vegetables.

Beef stew crumble (Brown stew)

"Many, many years ago one of the first dishes we made in cookery classes was a stew; easy for novices to make, but there was a twist, a crumble topping. At that young age, a savoury crumble was something I had never experienced. The gravy as a result of all the extra flour was thick and delicious. It has been cooked countless times since."

There are many recipes for savoury crumbles, but often these are vegetarian dishes with a gratin topping, rather than a full-blown hearty meal with proper crumble. Although it sounds strange, the topping works well, think of it as a large flat dumpling without the suet.

1lb steak and kidney
3 potatoes
2 carrots
2 onions
1 can oxtail soup
Salt and pepper
1 leek
1 pint stock

<u>Topping</u>

10oz plain flour
5oz butter
Pinch of salt

Fry the steak and kidney until sealed and browned then transfer to a heatproof dish. Peel and chop the vegetables and slice the leek, add these to the dish with the stock and the oxtail soup. Place the dish in a preheated moderate oven for about two and a half hours, the vegetables should be cooked through by then and the meat tender. Adjust the seasoning. Rub the butter into the flour until it resembles fine breadcrumbs, stir through a pinch of salt and sprinkle the topping on top of the casserole. Place it back in the oven for another half an hour until the crumble is golden brown.

Oxtail stew with dumplings

There is no getting away from the fact that poor man's food can be very flavourful, oxtail is no exception, dark, rich and beefy. Again, this is a recipe probably not developed in the Black Country, Spitalfields in London may lay claim to the UK first for oxtail, way back in the sixteen hundreds, now it often forms the basis for a traditional winter soup or stew. However, as oxtail has risen in popularity, so has the price. It is available from butchers and not difficult to find. If this is being sold pre-packaged, look for a mix of large and small sections, the smaller ones will be nearly all bone, with very little meat, but butchers, and rightly so, are reluctant to sell only the larger pieces as they are left with a glut of the smaller ones that people don't want to buy.

Oxtail is exactly that, the tail of an "ox" or cow to you and me, with whole tails weighing in at between 2lbs – 4lbs. The tail is skinned and chopped into rounds. Each ring of oxtail will have a central bone and juicy meat around that which will cook down into meaty, gelatinous rounds.

Slow Cooker Oxtail

1 ½ lbs oxtail
½ turnip
2 onions
2 carrots
3 medium potatoes
2 tablespoons pearl barley
1 tablespoon Worcester sauce
2 tablespoons tomato puree
Oxo cube
Seasoning

Dumplings
4oz self-raising flour
2oz suet
Pinch flour
1 tablespoon parsley, finely chopped

Turn the slow cooker on and allow it to warm up for a few minutes, some people fry the oxtail in seasoned flour before putting it in the slow cooker, but this will work just as well without. Peel and chop all the vegetables and add these to the slow cooker, place the oxtail in with the vegetables and add the rest of the ingredients for the stew. Top up with water, put the lid on and cook for 8 hours or until the meat is tender. Stir occasionally in the first hour to make sure the pearl barley does not catch on the bottom.

To make the dumplings put the flour, salt and suet into a bowl and mix, stir through the chopped parsley, add enough water to make a soft dough. Flour the hands and break off small pieces of dough, roll them into balls and drop into the gravy to boil. Dumplings could be added about an hour before the end of the cooking time, these will also help thicken up the gravy. Serve with mashed potato.

Oxtail Soup

Another slow-cooked, put it on and let it cook, tasty winter staple.

2lb oxtail, skinned and cut into rounds by the butcher
Seasoned flour to coat plus one tablespoon to thicken
Knob of lard or dripping
1 onion
1 carrot
1 stick of celery
Bay leaf
2 tablespoons tomato puree
1 tablespoon Worcester sauce
2 pints stock
½ pint red wine

Coat the oxtail in seasoned flour and fry in the lard or dripping until browned on all sides. Carrot, onion and celery are the holy trinity of meat cookery, giving a lovely depth of flavour to the finished gravy. Peel and chop these finely, take the meat out of the fat and add the vegetables, fry on a low heat until softened and the onions are beginning to caramelise. Deglaze the pan with the wine. Transfer the meat, vegetables and the liquid to a heatproof casserole. Add the stock, bay leaf, Worcester sauce and tomato puree. Bring to the boil, then turn down the heat and simmer until the meat is tender, around two to three hours.

Strain the soup, pull all the meat from the bones, chop this and add back to the soup. Blend the remaining flour with a little of the soup in a cup, or with a little butter before adding to the soup. If you just add the flour to the soup, it will form lumps and be difficult to mix in, boil up again to cook the flour and thicken. Check the seasoning, ensure this is piping hot and serve.

If you want to reduce the fat, you could refrigerate overnight before adding the flour, then skim off the fat that sets on the surface before reheating and thickening the soup.

Corned Beef Hash

Towards the end of the week, the meat bought on the weekly shop would run low, but hungry bellies still needed filling until the larder was restocked on shopping day. A hash is a dish of chopped meat and vegetables; corned beef hash was quick to make from store cupboard staples and the contents of the vegetable rack. And the corned beef? It had to be Frey Bentos.

7 large potatoes, can be leftover or freshly cooked
1 large can corned beef
1 onion
Knob of lard
Seasoning

Peel and slice the onion, melt the lard in a frying pan and add the onion. Fry over a gentle heat until the onion begins to soften, add a pinch of salt. While the onion is frying, chop the corned beef and potato into small cubes then add them to the pan. Continue frying until hot all the way through, do not stir too often, you can also add a splash of Worcester sauce. When the mixture is hot all the way through, press down into the pan so the base browns and crisps, turn the mixture over and crisp the other side. Serve with a fried egg and brown sauce.

Lamb or Mutton

Nothing went to waste, mutton was more commonly eaten than today, but frugal recipes eked out every last bit of meat.

Sheep's Head

This former cheap belly filler would have been used to produce a stew that could have been stretched to last for two or three days, once the fill had been taken of stew, the next sheep's head may have been roast or used to produce a soup. There was meat in that head that was destined for the dinner plate no matter how it was cooked. Not often seen on butcher's slabs these days. They are available but you will probably have to order them, smaller than pig's heads these are easier to cook at home.

There is not as much meat as on a pigs head, but the cheek meat is good and fat under the skin browns the head well as it cooks and there is good flesh underneath the eyeball.

Odd isn't it, progress. Thirty years ago, women would think nothing of picking a sheep's head up from the butchers and carting it home on the bus. Can you imagine the looks you would get today if the bag split?

Roast Sheep's Head

Little preparation is needed for this. Salt the head, possibly add a few herbs, oregano or rosemary. Wrap the head in foil and roast at around 350°F, 180°C, 160°C fan assisted, for about an hour and a half. Check after an hour, but leave longer if better cooked meat is preferred. One more thing, position it nose down in the tray unless you fancy all those lovely nasal secretions running back into the head. Better out than in, as they say.

Stewed Sheep's Head

Wash the head, place in a pan with just enough water to cover. Throw in some herbs and season. Simmer gently until very tender, skimming off any scum that might appear on top. Remove the head from the water. Add a thinly sliced onion and a shredded white cabbage to the water the head was cooked in; simmer until the vegetables are tender. Make a custard of two egg yolks and a pint of milk and use this to thicken the liquid. Place the cabbage and onion mixture on a serving plate with a little of the liquid. Place the head on top. Sprinkle with salt and serve.

Neck of lamb stew with parsnips, onions, carrots and pearl barley

A rich warming stew, both wholesome and hearty, sweet neck of lamb thickened up with pearl barley and winter vegetables bubbling away on the cooker all afternoon waiting for dinner time to come around.

The smaller bones can migrate into the gravy along with bone fragments where the meat has been chopped, but it is worth the risk, take care small children don't find bones in their portions. Older folks may remember sucking on the bones to get the last vestiges of goodness out.

1lb neck of lamb
3oz pearl barley
2 onions, peeled and sliced
2 carrots, peeled and sliced
3 potatoes, peeled and cut into chunks
½ parsnip, peeled and cut into chunks
1pt stock
1 leek, white part only, sliced into rounds
Sprig of thyme
Bay leaf
Small piece of lard
Seasoned flour

Heat the lard in a frying pan or stove-to-oven dish. While the lard warms, coat the pieces of lamb in the seasoned flour. Fry these gently in the lard until browned, if using another dish to cook the stew, put the lamb into the dish then add the remaining ingredients and place on the heat, bring to a simmer, stirring occasionally for around twenty minutes. This will allow the pearl barley to swell; keep stirring occasionally to prevent this burning to the bottom of the dish. Transfer to a preheated oven (160°C) for a further two hours, stirring occasionally, by the time it's done the meat should be falling off the bones. Check the seasoning and serve with crusty bread to mop up the gravy.

Rabbit stew

Rabbits, wild rabbits, were free food, caught and brought home for tea. They also breed, well, like rabbits. Prolifically. They could be hutch kept in the garden and there are, no doubt, grown up children still traumatised at coming home after school to rabbit stew on the table and an empty hutch. Rabbit came into its own in the war years, supplementing the meagre meat ration.

A simple dish, cooked in one pot, rabbit has a smell of its own when cooking, not unpleasant, but rabbitty. The colour and texture are a bit like chicken and the flavour quite mild.

1 rabbit – jointed
2 rashers of streaky bacon, chopped
2 tablespoons flour, seasoned with salt and pepper
Knob of lard
2 sticks of celery, chopped
3 carrots, peeled and chopped
2 onions, peeled and sliced
Bay leaf
Sprig of thyme

1 pint chicken stock
½ pint cider
3 potatoes, peeled and cut into chunks
10 mushrooms peeled and sliced.

Coat the rabbit in the seasoned flour, heat the lard in an ovenproof or heatproof dish and fry the rabbit to brown it on all sides. Remove the meat from the pan, throw in the bacon, celery, carrots and onions, fry until soft and just starting to colour, add any seasoned flour left over and fry for a further minute or so, stirring so the flour does not burn. Deglaze the pan with some of the cider; stir well to remove any bits stuck to the pan. Add the stock, cider, bay, thyme and rabbit portions. Bring to the boil, then turn down the heat and simmer for one hour before adding the potatoes. Simmer for a further hour, the rabbit should be tender by now. Fry the mushrooms in butter then add these to the stew. Cook for a further 20 minutes. If the gravy is too thin, boil to reduce the liquid or mix a tablespoon of flour into a knob of butter and add this a bit at a time until the desired consistency is achieved. Season to taste.

Offaly versatile

"Stuffed udders; eyeballs – cut in half with the black centres removed; confit of gizzards; warm lambs tongues with ginger, mustard and cream; beef palates were once a delicacy."

"In parts the US there are bans on eating udders and lungs."

"Offal is not awful."

Offal, is not always the most visually appealing selection of meats, but empty purses and sharp appetites have a way of overcoming resistance. Tasty and cheap in comparison to other cuts, offal includes some of the most flavoursome parts of the animal, parts that would otherwise have been neglected and gone to waste, such as the liver, tongue, kidney, lung or brains – organ meats. Black Pudding may be, debatably, of northern origin but is traditionally made and eaten in the Black Country from pigs blood collected when the animal was slaughtered and with so many pigs there was a lot of blood to use. Stuffed cow's udder anyone? Boiled for a few hours and served sliced on bread and butter. No – well how about a lovely slice of windpipe?

Brains

"Brains smell awful, but it's the texture that wins you over, like a savoury marshmallow or thick whipped cream."

"Covered in seasoned flour then thrown in smoking hot olive oil. Or soaked in brine, then poached in milk before mashing."

These are a step too far for some; reportedly, they have an almost sweet, creamy flavour and a texture of lightly set blancmange. The mere thought makes some people shudder, others adore them. Although eaten by relatively few these days, brains are still available to buy but can be difficult to source in the UK. Specialist butchers are about who can provide calf, sheep, pig or goat brains from animals under one year old. Since the emergence of BSE in the 1980's sale of brains from sheep or cattle over one-year-old is banned in Britain. Brains, particularly lambs, may be available from Halal meat suppliers.

Pigs brains have a tendency to come with the rest of the head and extracting this rare delicacy from its casing can prove tricky. Chipping away at the skull is time-consuming and hard work, better to ask a friendly butcher to do this part for you. Small fragments of bone often manage to find their way into the soft tissue before cooking, so watch out for this when eating.

Having managed the hard part, finding and if necessary extracting the brain, the next question is what do you do with it? Brains lend themselves well to a variety of cooking methods, frying, poaching or roasting all working well.

The first time you try brains, you will experience two things. Firstly a brand new flavour. Secondly, now this is entirely different and may strike during the preparation. Looking down at that piece of offal in your hand, the realisation dawns that the insignificant organ with a consistency somewhere between whipped cream and blancmange cupped in your hand was once home to the thoughts, the emotions, the memory, the very essence of a living being. Scary thought.

Brains are better soaked before cooking. They can be soaked in milk or water but this should be for at least an hour, preferably several. This removes any residual flavours and if you agitate them well while in the soaking medium, this will help to remove any fragments of remaining bone. Unusually brains are often cooked twice, boiled or poached first, then possibly fried or roast. The pre-cooking helps to set the shape, but as they are so soft, they benefit from being served with or on something else to help support them, some people would cook them inside a muslin bag in boiling water to hold them together. Brains were often served on toast or with egg. This may have been chopped boiled egg or scrambled egg stirred through before bringing them to the table.

For those brave or foolhardy enough to try, there are a couple of recipes below. Maybe I'm missing the trick here.

Fried Brains

Brains
Water
Lemon juice
Seasoning
2 eggs
Flour
Breadcrumbs
Peppercorns (optional)
Butter

Soak the brains as described above for at least an hour, several if there is time. Peel off the membrane covering the surface. Slice the brains in half, remove the brain stems and any other parts you don't fancy eating. Place the brains in a pan and add enough water to cover them, add the juice of half a lemon and a pinch of salt. You can add a few peppercorns for more flavour at this point and even a bouquet garni, the thought of exotic herbs may seem alien to a Black Country garden but thyme and sage were commonly grown.

Bring to the boil then turn down the heat and simmer for around six minutes. Remove the brains from the poaching liquid and let them cool, this will make them easier to slice. Cut into chunks.

Coat each chunk in flour, then dip in egg and finally seasoned breadcrumbs. Melt the butter in a frying pan and fry the brains over a medium heat, turning once or twice, until golden brown. Serve with hot toast.

Simple Fried Brains with Scrambled Egg

Poach the brains as above. Heat butter in a frying pan. Flour the brains and add to the butter, fry for a couple of minutes. Crack one or two eggs into the pan and cook through until the brains are done and the eggs are scrambled. Adjust the seasoning and serve hot with toast.

Ox tongue

Tongue was a "special occasion meat," served thinly sliced on white bread at tea. Most commonly, it was ox tongue, but sheep or pigs tongues were also used. Ox tongue looked huge when I was a child, a great hunk of pink meat lying on the butcher's slab, ready for boiling. Generally, these were brined before purchase and were ready to go in the pan as soon as you got them home. Once cooked, the meat is soft and easy to eat, with a surprisingly high-fat content. As with all meat, there are many methods of preparing for the table. If the plan is to roast tongue, it is best to remove the skin first. Scald the meat in boiling water and peel off the rough coating before the meat goes into the oven.

Boiled, pressed tongue is ideal for sandwiches, this can be boiled in a pan, bearing in mind an ox tongue is large so the pan will need to be equally large and this will take a fair amount of time, around 3 hours or so.

<u>Method for pressure cooking ox tongue</u>

A pressure cooker is of suitable size and reduces cooking time considerably. Trim the tongue if this has not already been done by the butcher; remove any additional parts from the base that do not look as though they would eat well, e.g. glands, attached muscles, the small bone found at the root of the tongue. Rinse the organ and place in a pan of cold water. Bring to a simmer, and then change the water. Repeat, but bring to the boil this time. After 5 minutes skim off any scum rising to the surface, the water could be changed, but if there is not too much scum, season well, put the lid on the pressure cooker and boil for around an hour. A bay leaf or two, peppercorns, an onion or leek could be added to the cooking water for more flavour before you bring up to pressure, but sometimes less is more.

When the skin starts to blister the tongue is cooked. Remove it to a plate to cool and keep back a little of the cooking liquid. Roll up the tongue and place in a casserole dish, choose a size that is a tight fit so the meat needs to be squeezed in. A little gelatine could be dissolved in the reserved cooking liquid and some of this poured into the casserole dish around the tongue to give a set jelly around the meat. Place a plate smaller than the diameter of the casserole dish on top of the tongue and on top of that place a weight or some tins of beans to press the meat.

Leave in a cool place overnight, transfer to a plate so you can carve slices.

Liver

This soft, reddish-brown meat cooks in minutes, possibly quicker than microwaving a ready meal, there is flavour in buckets and if cooked properly it is a world away from the hard, greyish, grainy slabs of over-cooked liver served up as school dinners. With dishes such as liver and onions regaining popularity as a mid-week dish, it is no wonder the price of offal is creeping up. Lambs liver is tender and sweet, ox-liver incredible value but personal preference lies in between. Pigs liver represents exceptional value, the flavour is not too strong and it is universally available.

<u>Liver and onions</u>

Ask the butcher to slice and trim the liver before you take it home then virtually all the preparation is done. Heat a knob of lard in a pan, slice an onion and fry gently with a pinch of salt until it begins to caramelise, toss in the liver. Fry gently until just coloured through, don’t cook for too long or the liver will be hard. Stir a spoonful of flour into the fat in the pan and cook for a minute or two before adding enough boiling water to make a thick gravy. If you have boiled potatoes or vegetables to serve with the liver use the water from those to make the gravy, this will give more flavour. If it the gravy is too pale, add a drop or two of gravy browning. Taste and adjust the seasoning. Serve with hot mashed potatoes.

Faggots (Savoury Ducks)

"Mom used to do them in the little cake tins."

"Lots of shops sold faggots, you'd go along with your own bowl and the one carrying them could lick the gravy."

"The queue was always outside the chip shop door on Fridays when they'd got faggots and peas."

Inexpensive and with a strong flavour liver forms the basis for one of the most well-known recipes from the Black Country – Faggots, traditionally served with mushy peas. Although often thought of as a West Country dish owing to the popularity of a certain commercially available brand, faggots are possibly the original takeaway food in the Black Country where they have been available for well over a century, with some recipes dating back to the 1800s. Whole cottage industries grew up around this meatball with humble origins. Hundreds were produced in the home where women would make and sell them from Front Room Faggot Shops; people took their own jugs to buy what they wanted. When Friday faggots were on sale in chip shops, the queue would snake out of the door.

The word "Faggot" refers to a bundle as in sticks. Meats are minced up and rolled or bundled into a ball then wrapped in caul or kell as it is sometimes known. This thin, lacy membrane holds them together and some of the caul fat will melt into the surface of the faggot during cooking, browning this and enhancing the flavour of the finished product.

Caul is a fatty membrane lining the stomach and intestines in pigs and some other table animals. Very thin and largely transparent, veins of fat give it lace-like appearance. Wrapping the faggots in this helps to keep them moist as they cook. Not always easy to come by, if you are lucky a helpful butcher may find enough for a batch of faggots if you ask. However, on a recent trip, a request for a fry was met with confusion.

"We don't make faggots like that anymore," said the butcher, "I wouldn't know what to charge." Another illusion gone. Faggots are quite obviously not what they used to be, but no book of Black Country recipes would be complete without a recipe for these.

The term fry was used to describe the heart, liver, lungs and windpipe, the term pluck may also have been used.

Faggots and peas

Pigs fry if you can obtain one from the butchers

If not: Pigs liver
Lungs (sometimes called lights)
Heart
Bread
Sage
2 Onions
Caul membrane

If a whole fry can't be sourced, and in all honesty, there will probably be too much liver in this for most people, use about 1 ½lbs liver and a heart, it is not easy to get hold of lungs, but add around ½ lb if they can be found.

Put the caul fat to soak into a bowl of hot water. While this soaks, mince the meats. Put them all through a mincer, and then add 2 peeled and chopped onions, about four slices of bread and a few sage leaves. Season and mix. This should result in a soft mixture. Roll a tablespoonful of the mixture at a time into a ball and wrap each in caul. Put these on a baking tray. They can be cooked without the caul if necessary, leave them bare or lay some streaky bacon across the top before putting into the oven. Cook in a preheated oven

180°C, 350°F, Gas Mark 4 for around 40 minutes. Serve with gravy and peas.

Mushy Peas

Along with fish and chips, faggots are a dish traditionally served with mushy peas. Pea puree or mashed, boiled green peas can be served but are not the same beast at all. Proper mashed marrowfat peas are called for. These are purchased dried, they need overnight soaking and yes, you've guessed it, long slow cooking. On the other hand, you could buy tinned and use a fork.

8oz dried marrowfat peas
1 tsp bicarbonate of soda
Salt
Sugar
Sprig of mint (optional)

Place the peas in a large bowl; they will swell as they soak. Add the bicarbonate of soda and pour in enough boiling water to fill the bowl. Put aside overnight. Drain, rinse the peas and transfer to a large saucepan, add a pinch of salt and cover with cold of water, add the mint. Bring to the boil and cook for around half an hour, until the peas are soft and mushy, remove the mint, add a teaspoonful of sugar. If there is too much liquid, boil down until the peas are thick and mushy, mash with a fork if necessary. Taste and adjust the seasoning.

Faggots (II)

1lb fry, pig's liver, heart and lungs. (If you can't get hold of lungs, increase the amount of heart and liver).
1lb pork belly
2 onions, peeled and finely chopped
4 or 5 fresh sage leaves or ½ tsp dried sage
2 slices of bread
1 ½ pints chicken stock

Caul

Cut the meat into cubes and place in a pan of boiling water, boil for 10 minutes. Allow to cool, then mince the meat, the onions, sage and bread. Season and mix well to combine. Shape into balls and wrap in the caul membrane. Place in a baking tin and pour in the stock. Cook in a preheated oven at 150°C, 300°F, Gas Mark 2 for about one hour. Serve with mashed potatoes and mushy peas.

Chitterlings (also chicklings, chyttetlynges or chitlins)

"Mention chitterlings for dinner and people turn a particular shade of green and become very inventive with their excuses."

Every bit of the pig was used, but opinion is divided over this particular part of the anatomy. Chitterlings are the prepared and cooked small intestines of a pig. The bit of the innards where the pig digests the food and begins to turn it into waste. They may not be palatable to everyone but have been included in the diet for hundreds of years. Records of these being eaten go back as far as the fifteen hundreds. Although the term is now only used to describe pig's intestines, previously it has been used for other animals and even referred to poultry.

These can be time-consuming to prepare and if not properly cleaned there may be health implications, an added drawback is the smell during cooking which may not be entirely pleasant and stems generally from insufficient cleaning. The key to a more pleasant experience is to be thorough when washing out the lengths of intestines; generally, these are turned inside out so the process is more effective. If you want to eradicate the smell in the house completely while boiling these several methods have been suggested. Try adding a potato to the water, boiling a pot of vinegar at the same time to disguise the smell or putting a slice of bread on top of the pot, however, the most effective method by far is to cook them in someone else's house.

Opinion is even more divided over taste, revolting is one of the more polite descriptions, but others regard it with the highest aplomb. Chewy in texture, not unlike squid, with a fatty, innardy taste that perhaps has to be acquired. The large intestine is rumoured to have a better flavour, more porky, there is more substance to it, the fat more melting, yum.

As you may have guessed, the writer has tried neither small nor large intestine of the pig. That is not down to squeamishness, you understand, more a lack of availability. But there's time yet.

If you want to try these, but don't fancy cooking them yourself, they can be found in traditional butchers shops but are becoming more difficult to find.

Served cold with lots of salt, vinegar and mustard accompanied by thinly sliced bread and butter or fried with bacon. Some say fried others not, cleaned, soaked, boiled and left to cool. Or even roast. They were also stuffed and cooked as a tough sausage. Despite having has lost popularity in the UK, chitterlings or chitlin's, are enjoyed as soul food and still well-liked in the USA.

Once you have managed to source chitterlings, you have to safely prepare and cook these. They may carry bacteria that can transmit to humans, the same is true for all meat products, but some porcine bacteria may be able to cause illness in people so the intestines need to be thoroughly cleaned before you cook and eat them. Boiling is the first stage, put them in a large pan and bring to a rapid boil for five minutes to kill any bugs. Next rinse in fresh water and once cool enough to handle check through each piece and remove anything you would not want to eat, straw for example or partly digested contents from the tubes.

Rinse them well in clean running water, remove any trace of part digested matter; you do not want to finish eating what the pig had already started. Sometimes the intestines are cut into chunks before cooking, but tradition dictates they are plaited after cleaning but before boiling.

They can then be boiled again or fried.

Tripe

"This is yet another part of the inside of an animal I could not get to grips with, dad used to tuck in, potential mother-in-law used to bring honeycomb tripe, ready washed and pre-packaged from the supermarket in the 1980's, it was duly cooked, boiled as I remember and wolfed down with gusto – by the dogs. It's not the look of it, nor the smell of it, more the lack of flavour and the chewy texture that does or rather doesn't do it for me. Chewy may be an understatement, like chewing a rubber band. Make your own minds up on the delights of tripe, there are those who swear by it and it is very popular abroad, even considered by some to have aphrodisiac qualities."

"Dad loved tripe with onions, celery and cream in a thick white sauce."

"The smell was like an open sewer."

The stomachs of cow, pig or sheep can all be eaten as tripe, but in the UK, only tripe from the cow tends to be used. Cows are vegetarian, meaning they eat a lot of grass and a lot of grass takes a lot of digesting. To cope with all that roughage, cows have a very complicated digestive system with not one but four stomachs. Four stomachs equals four different types of tripe.

The first one is the rumen from which comes smooth or blanket tripe; reports of this have described it as slimy or sloppy, even having the texture of snot, yum. You may sense a little unease about this one, but eat it people did.

Next, comes the reticulum, from whence honeycomb tripe is obtained. I was fascinated by the look of it as a child, in all its creamy coloured glory. The feel of this is somewhere between velvet and cabbage leaf. Unique. Thankfully. Best eaten, they say, with lots of vinegar.

Stomach number three, the omasum, gives us book or Bible leaf tripe.

Last, but not least, is stomach number four, the abomasum, thankfully most people would have had their fill of tripe before this because the lining of this stomach is glandular, this is where rennet is obtained (see Junket recipe), although it is eaten in other countries, the tendency is not to in the UK.

Green tripe, uncleaned tripe, so beloved of tripe hounds, is entirely recognisable by its colour and smell. It reeks of the end product of digestion, even after cooking. This is not a smell encouraging a healthy appetite as it wafts up from the dinner plate, and although consumed with gusto outside the UK, in my view best avoided for human consumption – ask the dog.

Four stomachs, now that's a lot of tripe.

These days the tripe you buy will generally have been prepared for the table, ready bleached, but a few years ago, a lot of the work would have to be done at home, the beasts would have been culled and the innards removed. The stomach would then need to be cleaned and cleaned thoroughly; you would not want to finish off the cow's last meal, would you? Dirt can hide well in those pockets of honeycomb so this was not a task to be taken lightly, but by thorough washing and cleansing in lots of changes of water, the taste will be cleaner than in commercially bleached products, I am not suggesting you by raw unbleached tripe, just saying.

I fear I may be doing this anomaly of the culinary world an injustice, tons and tons of the stuff has been consumed for years and years. It must have something going for it to have been a dinner table staple for all this time, and in all honesty, some people love the stuff, perhaps I just haven't tried hard enough. Tripe can be versatile, lacking in flavour of its own, it readily takes up the flavour of other ingredients and low, slow cooking makes it less chewy. And remember, there are many ways to cook tripe, boiling, frying, braising… Anyway, ladies and gentlemen, I give you tripe, the marmite of the meat world.

Tripe and onions

1lb tripe

2 large onions
1 pint milk
2oz butter
2oz flour
Salt and pepper

Cut the tripe into 1" squares and put it in a pan of cold water, bring to the boil and cook for about 15 minutes, empty the water out, swill the tripe and the pan and replace the water with the milk. Peel and slice the onions, add these to the milk and season. Bring to the boil and cook until tender, this could take around two hours. In another pan melt the butter, stir in the flour and cook for a couple of minutes over a low heat, gradually stir in the milk the tripe was cooked in and continue to cook until the sauce thickens. Add the tripe and the onions to the sauce to reheat and serve.

If you cannot face eating that all over blandness, you could dip the tripe in egg and breadcrumbs after it has been boiled, and fry it. Or you could even cook it in a rich ragout of tomato, garlic and olive oil.

Heart

The seat of the soul, or at least a tasty treat!

Stuffed heart was a popular dish. Hearts were often sold as animal food; they were cheap and easily available and in our house were often boiled to feed the dogs. Nevertheless, they smelt good, and they didn't look too bad either with their lean, tender meat. Well, you have to slice off a little, to test it; it might be bad for the dogs. It's at that precise moment when the meat hits your taste buds that you realise why they were so fond of hearts years ago. Never underestimate the heart; it is the most amazing organ and fully deserving of our total respect. It begins beating not long after conception, well before birth and beats continually until the day we die, never asking for a rest or a holiday, nor does it complain, lub dub, lub dub, the beat goes on.

The meat itself is lean aside from a layer of fat on the outside, close grained and reminiscent of steak.

They say you can die of a broken heart, so as you look at that small piece of loveliness on the plate, respect the heart and treat it well; alive or braised.

4 lamb's hearts
1 pack of parsley and thyme stuffing
3 sausages
4 – 6 rashers of bacon
1 onion
1 carrot
1 stick of celery
Lard
1 tablespoon flour
1 pint of stock

Trim the hearts, remove any fatty parts and tubes, in fact, anything that looks gristly, you could ask your butcher to do this part for you. Skin the sausages and add them to a bowl, sprinkle in the stuffing mix and add the amount of boiling water stated on the pack, enough to make a soft mix. Stir well to blend in the sausage and use this to stuff the hearts. Or, of course, you could make the stuffing yourself from scratch. Wrap each heart in bacon.

Slice the carrot, onion and celery thinly and fry gently in the lard until soft and the onions are beginning to caramelise, transfer to a casserole dish. Add the hearts to the frying pan and fry, turning until coloured all over then put these in the casserole dish with the vegetables. Add the flour to the frying pan (you may need to add a little more fat) and fry until the flour is cooked, gradually add the stock to make a gravy, pour this into the casserole with the hearts and put into a preheated oven at 160°C for around an hour and a half. Check and adjust the seasoning to taste. Serve with mashed potato.

Pig's hearts

These are roughly the same size as human hearts, makes you think doesn't it, this fist size chunk of muscle beats relentlessly keeping the animal alive. Once it stops its curtains. These are just as good for eating as sheep hearts. Cook it long and slow to tenderise or cook it quickly. Trim off the tubes and fat, open the heart up so it will lie flat, season the outside, rub it with olive oil and grill or flash fry.

Ox hearts

These are huge and again they make good eating if treated right, very high in protein and a palatable flavour reminiscent of steak. They do need careful trimming, slice the heart in half lengthways and remove the fat from the outside and top of the heart, don't worry if some of the meat comes away with this. The tubes at the top that poke out to each side also need to go, as do the two flaps at the tops of the heart. These were known as "deaf ears" as they resemble the ears on a pig. Remove any obvious arteries or other vessels and the heartstrings inside, along with anything else that feels tough.

Stuff and roast the heart for a traditional old English dish little seen nowadays. Given the size of the heart this will take a while, some recipes recommend anything up to five hours to slow roast, but the slow cook will tenderise the meat. You could use a forcemeat stuffing or something lighter such as bacon, mushrooms and onion, fried to soften these first.

Place one-half of the heart on a plate, on top of a length of butcher's twine. Fill this with the stuffing, then place the other half on top and tie it in place with the twine.

Heat a little fat in a frying pan and brown the heart before transferring to a preheated oven, 160°C, for about an hour, aim for 15 – 20 minutes per pound and don't overcook, the heart should still be pink and juicy. Once out of the oven allow the meat to rest before slicing as you would any other joint. Serve as you would a roast dinner.

Heart would be an interesting choice for a valentine meal, “I give you my heart.”

Pork Scratchings

There is no getting away from the fact that a pig is a large animal, and a large animal is covered by a lot of skin, which is generally sold on the joint of meat it covers. Competition is hot to produce the best crackling, crisp and golden adorning roast pork. There are other uses for pork skin and almost everyone in the Black Country will have heard of the pork scratching. This heart attack in a bag is believed to have originated from the region, which given the number of pigs co-existing with households makes this a distinct possibility.

Frequently sold as pre-packaged as snacks; the skin is cut from the pork, cleaned of hairs and rendered down. After cooking, the skin can be hard and has been responsible for many broken teeth, underneath there may be a softer fatty layer. Leaf fat from around the kidneys was boiled, producing a softer, crispy product, much easier on the teeth. High in salt and high in fat, they may not be the best health option but from humble beginnings as a snack for the working classes, scratchings have risen to near-iconic status today. Pork scratchings remain a firm favourite with millions of bags sold every year. They are one of the finest accompaniments to a pint of beer, brewed in the Black Country.

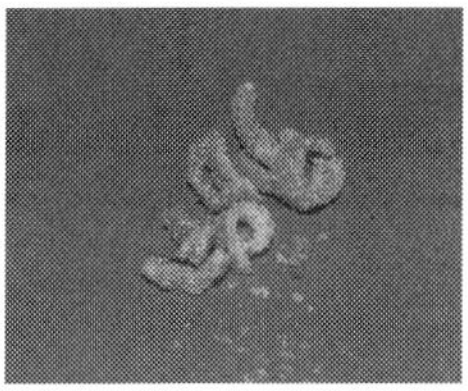

Who actually ate the first scratching is lost to the mists of time, but anecdotal evidence of them being prepared in the Black Country and surrounding districts dates back as far as the 1800s showing they have been popular for 200 years at least.

Black pudding (Pigs pudding, blood pudding, blood sausage)

There is little waste on a pig, even the blood makes a tasty sausage and there is a fair amount of blood contained inside the animal. Put yourself in the position of the slaughter man hundreds of years ago faced with the dilemma of what to do with the crimson lifeblood as this seeps away and is lost. What a waste he must have thought. Blood does not keep well, degrading quickly.

Also inside the pig is the ideal packaging system, yards of intestines, offering the perfect container for liquid blood. As early as 1500BC humans devised the method of using these natural casings to hold and cook the blood, setting it into a blood sausage, prolonging the shelf life and producing a nutritious food.

Since then, the recipe has been developed and refined to the product enjoyed today, there are national even regional variations, but in the UK, traditionally black pudding was made from pig's blood, oat or barley groats, usually barley, possibly pearl barley; pork fat, flavourings, seasonings and flour. It would have been simmered, not boiled - exploding puddings are difficult to sell, for around 25 minutes, producing a set, cooked sausage.

It may come as a surprise to learn the contents have changed. Pig's blood may not be present at all. Pigs, understandably, may not be entirely comfortable with the thought of being slaughtered and have a tendency to urinate during the process, contaminating the blood and rendering it unfit for human consumption. For this and a variety of other health and hygiene reasons, fresh blood is classed as a high-risk product and often disposed of at the slaughterhouse rather than being processed into black puddings.

There have been gruesome variations from pigs blood as the main ingredient, Dr Michael Mosely prepared and tested a pudding made from his own blood on television, his verdict of the unique ingredient, well, it was black pudding. Stereotypically mad scientist, the arm flinging late Magnus Pyke, as a young man during the Second World War was employed as a food researcher, working for Frederick Marquis 1st Earl of Woolton (after who the Woolton Pie was named), at the Ministry of Food. One of the more notorious suggestions of young Magnus was to combat problems of storing the excess donated blood collected for transfusions. Rather than wasting this owing to the short shelf life, he suggested turning the surplus into black puddings. Literature does not make clear whether this was trialled, but it was wartime.

The main ingredient now comes in dried powder form, often from abroad, worse still it is not even from pigs, but often bovine in origin, with maybe a dash of lamb's blood thrown in for good measure. Even the casings may have been updated, if the black pudding purchased for breakfast now comes wrapped in plastic, remember to remove this, it won't taste nearly as good as the rest!

Flavourings vary from region to region, some use mace, others cayenne, possibly pennyroyal, the more northern the more studs of white fat the pudding contains, which incidentally some people reckon is the best bit.

Despite the grisly origins, no breakfast fry up would be complete without two or three crispy on the outside, soft on the inside, fat-studded, pearl barley flecked, crumbly black sausage slices. Black pudding is back on the menu.

Not many home cooks would consider whipping up a batch of pig's pudding from the raw ingredients – though there are the hardened few! A recipe has not been included here, but these are readily available and only a fingertip google search away.

Breakfast aside, this also works well on a sandwich with cheese and onion.

Easily available from any good butchers as either rings or thicker sticks. These puddings will have already been cooked so can be eaten as they are or they can be fried, grilled or baked in the oven if you prefer a crispier finish, further cooking has the advantage of melting the fat inside giving another aspect to the flavour. It also works very well as an additional layer in a Lancashire hotpot.

It's perfectly fowl

Fowl were an integral part of family life for many, helping to stretch the housekeeping to put food on the table. Chickens and ducks scratched contentedly in the garden, quietly clucking their way round the borders, providing eggs for the table and cockerels for the pot. When the hens were too old to lay, they too would be destined for the stew jar. Tough older birds would be casseroled or boiled. One hint for tenderising the meat was to bury the carcass in the garden for 24 hours before cooking. Immune systems must have been more efficient back then; this practice would not be recommended now.

Bantams were ideally suited to small spaces, true the eggs are smaller but as well flavoured as those from any of the larger breeds of chicken, and bantams have a character far in excess of their small size.

Life was sometimes hard, mothers would struggle to feed large families and underhand tactics were resorted to in times of need. Poaching was rife, rabbits, pigeons, whatever came to hand to fill the pot was fair game and chickens were not out of range. If reports in the Black Country Bugle are to be believed, in the 1800s Bilston was the chicken rustling capital of the Black Country, poultry pinching raids on neighbour's coops were commonplace, with hit lists being planned in the local pub over a pint of ale.

Along with chicken and ducks, there may have been a goose or two for Christmas. Backyard poultry keeping declined in popularity in the post-war years but chickens are once again infiltrating the gardens of suburbia.

"We had a cockerel once, big beast of a bird he was. Tall too. White feathers and speckled grey ruff of a Light Sussex, there should have been a cautionary notice stamped on his feathers, "approach with caution and preferably a broom handle." There was nothing lightweight about Sussex, and never any problems with foxes while he was about."

"Two dozen day old Black Rock chicks arrived to increase the flock, tiny balls of fluff that fit into the palm of your hand. A good way of settling young chicks was under a surrogate mum, otherwise known in the trade as a mop head. They would snuggle warm and cosy as if they were under a live hen. How incubator hatched chicks would know this is a mystery, but snuggle they did, chicks under the mop, mop under a lamp on the shelf in the lounge, all content. So content I went out, leaving them quietly growing under their mop. Two hours later, I remembered the cat was also comfortably sleeping in the same room. It is a well-known fact that cats like birds and our house cats were very good hunters. It was noted with extreme surprise, not to mention relief on arriving home, that there they all were, chicks still under the mop, the cat curled up next to them on the arm of the chair, an additional protective surrogate mother. Not a feather had been touched."

Roast duck is a wonderful dish, better perhaps for a visiting fox than for those who feed them every day when the duck is home grown. Difficult to enjoy every mouthful when the bird was hand fed in life, but ducks lay well and the eggs alone make them worth keeping.

Notes on roasting duck

Before cooking, salt the skin well and cook on a rack above a roasting tray allowing the fat to drip through. The skin should be crisp and golden, like very thin crackling. Perfect. The meat meltingly tender is darker than chicken with more flavour. This has a reputation for being fatty, true there is a lot of fat, but if cooked as above, most of the fat will be in the tin, not in the bird.

Parsons noses

Parsons noses could be brought without the rest of the turkey attached, and for those who don't know what the parson's nose is – look it up! Considered a delicacy by some, this can be very fatty but if properly roast, the fat is rendered out and the skin becomes crisp and golden.

Giblet pie

Old and practically forgotten now, giblet pie is hardly ever come across, years ago everything from poultry was used, including the bits of the bird that on a good day gravy is prepared from, occasionally stock or chicken liver pate. Years ago, cooks were far more adventurous.

The contents of the pie could have been goose giblets; this could then have been served with the cooked bird, or equally, may have been served as a meal in its own right. In the Black Country goose was expensive and often reserved for Christmas, even then it was considered too good for children who would more usually be offered roast rabbit. For this recipe, if you do not have access to goose giblets, those from a chicken could be used instead.

Giblets and the neck of the chicken or goose
1 onion, chopped
2 bay leaves
1 bunch of kitchen herbs (parsley, thyme etc. – but not mint)
Worcester sauce
4 fl oz double cream
Beef or lamb steaks – slices
Shortcrust pastry

Preheat the oven to 400°F, 200°C, 180°C fan assisted. Trim any unpleasant bits from the giblets, e.g. gall bladder, and boil the giblets, which should include the neck of the bird, the liver, heart, gizzard, and any other bits you have, with the onion, the herbs, the Worcester sauce and seasoning in a small amount of water. Turn the heat down and simmer for about half an hour. Take off the heat and remove the giblets from the stock. Strain the stock, this will be needed later. Line the bottom of a pie dish with the steak or lamb, the meat may need to be pounded first to flatten it. Remove any bones from the necks and any tough bits, membrane or sinew from the giblets. Slice them and place these on top of the meat, season. Add just enough stock to cover the meat. Roll the pastry out to fit the dish and put the crust on, brush with milk or beaten egg. Bodge a hole in the top of the crust to let the steam out and bake for around an hour until the pastry is golden and the meat is done. Remove from the oven, warm the cream then lift one side of the pie crust and stir in the cream.

Giblet gravy

This was always served at Christmas to accompany the turkey. Put all the giblets into a heatproof dish along with an onion, a bay leaf and seasoning. Cover with boiling water and put the dish in the oven with the turkey. Roast for about 45 minutes, until cooked.

Remove from the oven and put aside until the turkey is cooked. Pull as much meat from the turkey neck as possible and chop the rest of the giblets finely (if the gizzard is there you may want to leave this out). The giblets have a strong flavour; you may want to taste a little before adding them to the gravy and leave them out if you feel the taste is too strong. Remove the turkey from the tray and let the contents of the roasting tin rest for a few minutes, the fat will rise to the top making it easier to drain off most this into a cup (in case you need to add some back to make extra gravy). Put the roasting pan onto a low heat with the turkey dripping and a little of the fat, add a tablespoon of flour, stir over the heat for a few minutes, do not let this burn, add a little more fat if needed. Once the fat has browned, add the liquid from the giblets, scraping out any sediment from the bottom. Stir while it thickens; add the water from the vegetables and from the potatoes along with the giblet meat. If this is too pale, add a drop or two of gravy browning.

Gizzard

This is part of the digestive tract of a chicken, or pigeon, or pheasant… Just below the neck is the crop, a sort of bag where the bird accumulates food. Corn or green food is often found there when dressing a carcass. The food then passes through the digestive system until it reaches the stomach, located just behind this in chickens in the gizzard. There may be grit in the gizzard, which helps the bird to break down food. As you might expect even these parts of the bird were cooked and eaten.

For the brave few who would like to try cooking these, peel the inner membrane away and discard this, it will be bitter. Clean and remove any fat from the outside. The cleaning can take a while; there are crevices that must be washed out and plenty of them.

Once cleaned, fat and membrane removed, chop the gizzards into small pieces. In a small pan, fry a chopped onion and the gizzard meat. When the meat is cooked through, turn down the heat and add half a cup or so of water, put a lid on and simmer for 5 -10 minutes, checking to make sure this does not boil dry. Then turn the heat up and add one chopped fresh tomato or half a tin of tomatoes, continue to boil until the excess liquid is reduced, season well, add half a teaspoon of sugar, a tablespoon of tomato puree, a tablespoon of chopped coriander and a dash of sweet chilli sauce.

Rook pie

A popular dish if you would believe wartime propaganda from WWII when rooks could be used to supplement meagre meat rations. Four and twenty blackbirds baked in a pie and all that. This was made with rooks – not crows. Crows eat dead things – carrion, which does not generally sit comfortably with English tastes. “Brancher” rooks are young and tender having just left the nest, they are still unable to fly. Much better in a rook pie.

When you have acquired enough rooks to fill a pie dish, cut off the breasts, you can use the legs as well but there is barely enough meat on these to make it worth the effort. Place the rook on its back, slit the skin and peel this back exposing the breast meat. Cut the breast from the carcass with a sharp knife. Chop an onion, a carrot and some celeriac, toss these into a frying pan and fry until the onion is soft, then sear the breasts in the pan along with some chopped streaky bacon. You could also add some chopped chicken breast or steak. Season, add a bay leaf and a sprig of thyme, then pour in half a pint of good stock and simmer for half an hour.

While the meat is simmering line a pie dish with pastry, puff pastry works well, but you could also use shortcrust. Drain the meat and transfer to the pie dish, add four hard boiled eggs cut into quarters. Thicken the gravy and add to the pastry case leaving about ½" at the top. Add a lid, press down to seal, cut a hole in the top to left the steam out, bake at 180°C until the pastry is golden, and cooked through. Serve with mashed potatoes and veg and extra gravy as required.

Pigeon (Squab)

With huge populations of pigeon frequenting almost every town centre, it would be reasonable to expect these to appear in butchers with alarming regularity. Sadly, this is not the case. Pigeons can be difficult to source, which is a shame, as they are tasty birds. They have graced dinner plates for many years, particularly during meat rationing in the Second World War when they were plentiful and easy to obtain, but seem to have fallen from favour somewhat now.

Pigeons are small, there is no getting away from that, one bird is not a family meal, the breast is really the only part worth eating. Slightly darker than chicken and tougher but not so very different in flavour, a little drier and a little more flavoursome.

They can be roast whole, after plucking and dressing obviously or the breast can be removed and cooked separately. However they are cooked, pigeon is worth trying.

The meat is healthy with very little fat, but the downside to this is that they can dry out during cooking, so cook fast and hot. The best time to buy wild pigeon is between September and November when they will generally be at their fattest.

Roast Pigeon

At least one bird per person. Young birds are more suitable for roasting.

Season the birds with a little salt and pepper. Flash fry, searing all sides in a pan, paying attention to the legs and wings, these should be partly cooked when the birds go into the oven. Aim for around six minutes in the pan. Don't cook the breast long or it will be overdone after roasting. Then transfer to the roasting tin and cook in a preheated oven, 180°C fan assisted, 200°C or Gas Mk 6 for about 10 – 12 minutes for rare meat or 15 -18 minutes for well done. Rest the birds for 5 minutes before serving. Works well with roast vegetables, carrots, potatoes, celeriac (parboiled), onion, sweet potato, splashed with oil, sprinkled with sea salt and put into the hot oven some time before the pigeon, as in this recipe the vegetables will take considerably longer to cook than the meat.

Pigeon Breast

Grill with butter or flash fry and serve on a bed of caramelised onions, mushrooms and bacon, add a pepper sauce or port and redcurrant jelly sauce and all is right with the world.

To remove the breast, put the bird on its back and pierce the skin with the tip of a sharp knife, if the pigeon is still feathered there is no need to pluck if you are only using the breast meat. Peel back the skin exposing the flesh, slice along the breastbone, following the bone down with the point of the knife work down and back, removing the breast meat from one side in one piece, then repeat on the other side of the breastbone. Rinse and pat dry with kitchen towel.

Slice an onion and fry slowly in a knob of butter with a dash of oil added to stop it burning. Add a pinch of salt, which will help to draw the water out, when the onion is soft add a pinch of sugar and fry until soft and golden. While the onions are cooking, slice a handful of peeled mushrooms and a chop rasher or two of bacon. Remove the onion from the pan and turn up the heat, throw in the mushrooms and bacon, fry for three or four minutes until the mushrooms are tender and browning remove these and put with the onions.

Season the pigeon breasts and fry for three or four minutes a side, less for really rare, a little more if they are preferred cooked through.

A minute before they are done put the onion mixture back in the pan to heat through.

Serve the pigeon on a bed of onions and mushrooms, accompany with mash, chips, or whatever.

Vegging out

"I have to make sincere apologies to all my vegetarian friends for the brevity of this section. It would seem in the past Black Country folk were a carnivorous bunch. The few recipes that keep cropping up are largely based on ways of using up leftovers, but they still taste great."

Bubble and squeak

Anything goes here; all the vegetables left over from a roast dinner went into the frying pan the following morning to produce a savoury cake of deliciousness with a golden, crispy bottom. Potato was the main ingredient, mashed or boiled into the frying pan it went, cabbage is another stalwart of bubble and squeak, but it really does not matter carrots, sprouts or any leftover veg can be used. Onion, gently fried in lard or any leftover dripping until it caramelises is a good base, then add everything else. Pack the veg down into the pan and do not be too quick to turn it, a good crispy brown bottom cannot be beaten, flip it over, does not matter if it all breaks up and brown the other side. It's as simple as that. Some people shape it into little cakes, like fishcakes, other people make one big bubble and squeak cake. Any shape works, it's the taste that counts.

Bubble and squeak can be served as part of a breakfast or with a couple of rashers of crispy bacon or even a fried egg.

And if you ever wondered how it got its name, you have never cooked it! Listen to the sounds coming from the pan while it fry's and all will be revealed.

Cheese and potato pie

Yet another comfort food dish that could be prepared from leftover potatoes. Popular with children, ideal when the cupboards, not to mention the bank, are running low. The crispy bits around the edge of the dish are highly prized together with the soft stringiness of the melted cheese.

Leftover cooked potato – enough to fill the dish you have in mind, or peel and boil about eight medium size potatoes.
1 onion
Butter
Milk
Salt and pepper
8 tablespoons of grated cheese, ideally strong cheddar, something with a bit of bite
1 tomato

If you are not using leftover mash, mash the potatoes, add a splash of milk and a knob of butter, you won't need too much butter, as there is plenty of fat in the cheese. Caramelised onion adds extra flavour. Thinly slice the onion and fry gently, as it begins to soften add a little salt to draw the water out and fry until it is soft and translucent, give it a few minutes longer until the onion starts to brown. Don't skimp on the cheese, add plenty, it is a cheese and potato pie after all, so you should be able to taste the cheese. Mix half of the cheese into the potato and season well, place half into an ovenproof dish. Spread the onion over this and sprinkle over a handful of the remaining cheese, so you have a layer in the middle. Top with the remaining potato, then the last of the cheese. Slice the tomato thinly and arrange over the pie. Cook in a moderate oven,

180°C for about twenty minutes, until the cheese on top is melted and bubbling, the potato starting to brown and the tomato is cooked. Eat on its own or serve with a side salad.

Red Cabbage

Savoury, piquant and sweet, this is great with just about anything. Ruby red cabbage glistening with butter, sweet with apple and sharp with vinegar, strange but delicious. Many recipes include onion, if you want to add onion, heat a knob of butter with a drop of oil to prevent it burning, in a deep frying pan, add a thinly sliced onion, season and fry gently until soft, then add the red cabbage and carry on as per the recipe.

½ red cabbage
2 tablespoons soft brown sugar
1 onion (optional – see above)
1 cooking apple
Butter
Vinegar

Remove the wilted, tough outer leaves from the cabbage and discard, cut the cabbage in half, then slice into shreds, discarding the tough internal ribs. Place into a large, deep frying pan with just enough water to cover. Add a knob of butter and put on a medium heat. Peel the apple and slice into the pan, season. Add the sugar and 3 tablespoons of vinegar. Cook until the cabbage is soft adding more water as necessary. It will take at least half an hour before the cabbage is soft, taste at intervals, add more sugar or vinegar as necessary, there should be plenty of flavour in the dish. Stir in another knob of butter before serving. This reheats well and is possibly better the following day.

Egg Fry (Eggy Bread)

Not vegetable based, but still vegetarian. Crispy egg fried bread may seem a strange choice for a regional cookbook, but enquiries about recipes and foods people associated with the area repeatedly brought forth eggy bread, so here it is. The breakfast of childhood or lean times when a full English was priced out of reach.

Day old, slightly stale bread, as many slices you can manage
2 large eggs
2 tablespoons of milk
Pinch of salt
Knob of butter
Oil

Heat the oil and butter in a frying pan, the oil will stop the butter burning. Beat the eggs and the milk together, dip the bread in the egg and milk mixture, turn it over and dip the other side, allow the excess to drip off, back into the egg mixture then sprinkle a little seasoning on the bread. Fry for two or three minutes a side until crispy and golden. You could serve this on its own, as part of a breakfast, with yoghurt and fruit (completely untraditional) or with a sprinkling of sugar and cinnamon.

Swede 'n' tatas (Neeps and tatties)

Traditional Burns Night fare north of the border, but anytime will do in the Black Country, works well with liver and onions or belly draft.

1lb swede
1lb potato
Salt and pepper
Knob of butter
Dash of milk
Nutmeg

Put a pan of boiling water on the hob. Peel the swede and chop into 1cm chunks, put this on to cook, give it a ten-minute head start on the potatoes. While this is boiling, peel and chop the potatoes and add to the pan. Salt the water and cook until tender. Drain. This can then be roughly chopped with a sharp knife, season and add a knob of butter before serving. If you prefer a smoother dish, mash as you would potatoes, add a splash of milk, a knob of butter, season and serve.

Carrot and turnip.

Cook as above – peel and chop the veg into 1cm cubes, boil and chop or mash with a knob of butter.

Whole stuffed onions

An onion could provide a meal. Dubious? Work with me here. Spanish onions, if you can get them are mild and sweet, crisp and juicy but the idea of eating a whole one and nothing else is not entirely pleasant. Consider then roasting an onion as you would in the tin around or under the Sunday joint. They become so meltingly soft and sweet that you can spread them like butter. Wonderful. But not on their own for a whole meal. Boiled then, like the onions for a hot dog, but boiled whole. A large onion, naked of its skin, boiled until tender and all the bitterness gone. Getting better now? Still need more? Read on.

1 large onion, peeled, per person
Bacon
Fresh breadcrumbs
Cheddar – grated
Mushrooms
Seasoning
Knob of lard
1 chopped sage leaf
Stock

The amounts suggested should be sufficient to stuff four onions. Boil the onions for around 8 minutes until the outer layers are softening, you can leave them longer. Remove from the water and leave to cool. Meanwhile chop 2 rashers of bacon and about twice as many mushrooms as you think you will need, about 4oz, possibly more. Slice the top off the onions and remove the centres. Leave a good shell, thick enough to stuff and roast. Chop some of the removed onion finely. Heat a little lard in a pan, add the chopped onion and fry until starting to soften and colour, throw in the bacon, then the mushrooms and sage. Stir for a few minutes until the bacon is cooked. Remove from the heat and transfer to kitchen roll to drain, then transfer to a bowl, mix in the grated cheese and a tablespoon or two of breadcrumbs. Season and stuff the onions. Pack these into a shallow ovenproof dish, sprinkle cheese over the top and pour in stock to a depth of about an inch around the onions, cover the dish with foil. Bake for about three-quarters of an hour, basting as and when needed to ensure the onions don't dry out. They should be soft and tender when done.

Puddings – Desserts sounds too airy fairy, the puddings of the Black Country were substantial affairs

Puddings were a serious affair, often highly calorific comfort food based on whatever was to hand. Most gardens had fruit trees, apple, pear and damson, sometimes elder or mulberry. There were currant and gooseberry bushes, strawberries and raspberries in summer. This gave rise to a wide variation of puddings, pies, jams and other fruit based desserts.

Wild fruit was gathered in autumn, blackberries, sloes, crab apples and elderberries, there were nut trees in the hedgerows and if all else failed scrumping in someone else's orchard was a popular pastime.

Other puddings made use of leftovers, bread pudding for example, and its lighter cousin bread and butter pudding.

Some were thought to aid the recovery of convalescents; egg custard was widely regarded as an invalid food, soft and easy to eat but full of protein and calories.

There would be cake for high tea. Tinned fruit, reserved for special occasions accompanied by thinly sliced bread and butter. Tinned peaches served with carnation milk, also from a tin, was indeed a treat.

"As a child, I hated the skin on bright orange tinned peaches, but the syrup was lovely. I'd pour carnation milk in from a jug, so thick it didn't mix with the syrup. The peaches were always served from a fancy bowl at the table, using the big serving spoon the shape of a shell."

Milk Puddings

Time was often at a premium fifty years ago. More labour saving devices were available than to previous generations, but this was before the development of microwaves and food processors, freezers were just making their way into homes of the select few and convenience foods weren't even a blip on the horizon.

Milk puddings were a cheap, simple way to round off a meal. Ingredients were few, preparation time was short and they would cook in the oven alongside the meat. Short, fat, hard grains of rice transformed into a soft, creamy pudding was culinary magic at its most simple.

Semolina, rice, macaroni and tapioca frogspawn were all variations on a theme. A spoonful of jam or stewed fruit dolloped on top to give an extra dimension.

Pudding rice or short-grain rice gives the traditional rice pudding texture, a great winter warmer to combat the cold nights.

Rice pudding

4 rounded tablespoons of short-grain rice
2 pints whole milk. (You can substitute some of this with a can of evaporated milk)
5 tablespoons sugar
Nutmeg
Butter

Set the oven at low to warm up, Gas Mk 2 or around 150°C or if you are lucky enough to have use of an Aga or Rayburn pop this in the bottom oven overnight or first thing in the morning. Try to stir it once or twice through the cooking time or it may be thick enough to slice when done. It helps to warm the milk in a pan on the stovetop first, then stir in the rice and sugar bringing to a simmer before pouring into an ovenproof dish, but you don't even really need to do that if you're feeling lazy. The whole lot could go straight into the cooking dish, just stir well to mix thoroughly. A tin of carnation milk could be added for extra richness. Dot the top with butter and a generous grating of nutmeg and put into the warm oven.

Allow at least two hours to cook for rice pudding and stir it once or twice while it's cooking to prevent it becoming lumpy. The longer you leave it the thicker it will become and a golden brown skin will form on the top, which some people believe is the best part.

If it looks as though it is getting too thick while it cooks, add a drop more milk to thin it down. There are those who prefer their rice pudding thick enough to slice, which is all too easily achievable with a little lack of attention.

Flaked rice, ground rice and semolina puddings.

These are all quicker to cook and just as simple to prepare as baked rice pudding, they can be cooked in the oven in the same way, again stir during cooking, or you could end up with a pudding resembling gloopy wallpaper paste. If you are in a hurry all of these can be cooked in a pan on the stovetop, you will not get the brown, crispy skin but you will save a considerable amount of cooking time. For a little variation, you could serve with jam or flavour with cocoa or drinking chocolate.

Flaked rice sometimes comes ready-flavoured as strawberry or chocolate, but can be more difficult to find than ground rice or semolina. It does not seem to thicken quite as much during cooking either.

3 tbsps semolina, ground or flaked rice
3 tbsps sugar (or to taste)
1 ¼ pints milk
Butter
Nutmeg

Place semolina, ground or flaked rice into a pan with the milk and sugar and heat gently until simmering. Stir to make sure it does not catch. You can either carry on cooking on the stovetop, stirring until thickened (about twenty minutes), or transfer to a dish and finish in a low oven. Dot the top with butter and grate over a little nutmeg before it goes in. Stir once or twice, it will not take as long as rice pudding, 40 minutes should be plenty, again it will thicken as it cooks so keep an eye on it and check from time to time.

Sago and tapioca puddings

Sago and tapioca are both starch based, dried round balls that form the basis of a sweet milk pudding. Sago is made from the pith of the Sago palm tree, tapioca from the root of the cassava plant, but the taste is very similar, and they are interchangeable in pudding recipes. They can be cooked in just the same way as a baked rice pudding, the sago and tapioca will turn clear as they cook, giving rise to the alternative name of frog spawn. Check the packs for cooking instructions as some need soaking overnight which is simple enough to do, but generally, the packs of sago and tapioca bought in the UK can be used straight from the pack.

A slightly different version is shown below, a sort of sago queen of puddings.

2 or possibly 3oz sago
2 pints whole milk
4oz sugar
Vanilla extract
Pinch of salt
Nutmeg
Knob of butter
2 Eggs
Apricot jam
Additional 4oz sugar for the meringue

Set the oven to about 150°C. Warm the milk, sago, sugar, vanilla and a pinch of salt, stir to make sure they don't catch. Simmer until the sago is cooked, you will see it turn from solid balls to transparent. Add a generous knob of butter and a grating of nutmeg and stir. Take the pudding off the heat. Separate the eggs, then beat the yolks and mix into the pudding. Transfer to an ovenproof dish. Put small spoonful's of apricot jam across the surface of the pudding – not too much but enough to give it flavour. Whisk the egg whites to stiff peaks, gradually whisk in the additional sugar a little at a time. Spread the meringue over the surface of the pudding, pulling the surface into peaks.

Bake for around 45 minutes, until the meringue is crisp and golden brown.

Macaroni pudding

This is a pasta-based pudding, again very similar to rice pudding and cooked in a similar way.

6oz macaroni
1 pint milk
2 or 3oz Sugar
Knob of butter

Cook the macaroni as normal in boiling water until tender, approximately ten minutes. Preheat the oven to 160°C. Add the cooked macaroni to an ovenproof dish, pour the milk over, stir in the sugar and dot with butter. Grate over some nutmeg and transfer the pudding to the oven. Bake for around 40 minutes to an hour until the top is golden.

Alternatively, you could cook the macaroni and transfer to the dish, beat two eggs with the sugar and milk, pour over the pasta. Dot with butter, grate over nutmeg and bake as before.

Baked Egg Custard

Another pudding evoking fond memories of childhood, warm, comforting with a soft hit of vanilla, silky smooth, and easy to eat, so easy to eat it was considered as an ideal food for invalids. An added bonus is that it is a doddle to make. You can pour the mix into a pastry case to produce an egg custard tart but it is just as good naked. Long, slow cooking is best with the custard baked sitting in a hot bath to prevent it splitting. Take care not to cook in an overly hot oven or the result will be sweetened scrambled egg.

1 pint whole milk – you can substitute some of this for cream
3 eggs plus one egg yolk
2 ½ heaped tablespoons sugar
Vanilla essence

Preheat the oven to 160°C and put the kettle on to boil. Scald the milk and sugar in a pan, do not let it boil, stir to dissolve the sugar. Meanwhile beat the eggs and egg yolk with the vanilla essence, not too much; you don't want it to become frothy. Pour the hot milk into the eggs and stir to mix.

Strain into a heatproof dish and add a grating of nutmeg over the top. Put a roasting tin in the oven and three-quarters fill with boiling water, stand the pudding in the roasting tin, the water should come halfway up the sides of the pudding dish. Alternatively, use ramekin dishes for individual puddings.

Cook for around 35 minutes until set, depending on your oven this could take longer, don't rush it, aim for a finished product that still has a bit of a wobble.

This is good mouth burningly hot, straight out of the oven or served at room temperature after it has been left to set. You could serve with a portion of berries or stewed fruit.

Milk Jelly

Very few people do not remember the simple pudding of milk jelly from childhood, plunging the spoon into the softly resisting depths. As easy pudding with one simple caveat, you have to remember to let the jelly cool before adding the milk to avoid ending up with a curdled mess.

1 block of jelly – your favourite flavour
1 large tin carnation milk

Break up the jelly into a Pyrex jug and add half a pint of boiling water, stir until the jelly has dissolved. To save a little time you can break up the jelly into the jug, add a couple of tablespoons of water and give it a short blast in the microwave to melt, and then add cold water. This way the jelly will cool more quickly. When cold add the carnation milk, stirring as you do. The can could be placed in the freezer or fridge for a while first. Then top up the jug with cold water to the one-pint mark. Pour it into the mould and let it set. Turn out to serve. If this curdles, most likely this is because the jelly was too hot when the milk was added.

Milk Jelly Mousse (Jelly Fluff)

Put the can of evaporated milk in the fridge or freezer, but not long enough to freeze. Make up the jelly in a Pyrex jug as described above, using about half the water stated on the pack and allow it to cool. Whisk the evaporated milk until thick, whisk in the jelly and pour into the mould to set. Hey presto Milk Jelly Mousse.

Trifle

High days and holidays, there was always a trifle. Always a sherry trifle. There are nearly as many variations of trifle in the Black Country as there are women to make it, and each firmly believes theirs is best. Which type of jam? Is there alcohol? Which one? What toppings are added? Should there be fruit? The list is endless – well almost.

The not-quite Mother-in-Law always used to put a layer of jelly and fruit in the bottom. Firm set strawberry jelly, a bright red layer under the custard, with the fruit set into the jelly. This felt alien, at home trifles always followed the tradition of sponge, custard, cream and of course, alcohol; then pastel coloured hundreds and thousands scattered over the top. Hundreds and thousands - hard bits! Too crunchy spoiling the overall soft, squidgy body of the trifle – why would anyone add hard bits?

Trifle must have alcohol and it should be sherry, unless there is none, in which case port can be substituted, just tell everyone it's sherry. If there are children present, orange or apple juice can be exchanged for the alcohol, but the result does not constitute a proper old school trifle.

Trifle sponges (homemade sponge or bought trifle sponge, or even ratifa biscuits but not boudoir biscuits – these are for Charlotte Russe!)
Jam - strawberry
Sherry
Brandy
Sugar
Vanilla extract
Custard
Cream
Something to decorate (flaked almonds, hundreds and thousands, crushed flake bars, cherries etc.)

Butter the sponges with jam, any jam will do as long as it's tasty. Strawberry or raspberry are traditional, but apricot, damson or a whole variety of others have been used, whatever is left in the pantry works well. Place the sponges in the bottom of a pretty bowl and drown in sherry. Plenty to cover and a drop for luck. Pour in what you think will be too much, then add another drop; trifle sponges are thirsty things and will soak it all up.

Now the tricky bit. Do you make your own custard or are you a lazy beggar like me, who has tinned or carton custard hidden behind the baked beans in the pantry? Ready-made will do and sometimes has a better flavour than homemade.

Mum would turn in her grave at ready-made custard, which gives a much softer finish with no clearly defined layers. It is grudgingly admitted that a proper trifle should have well-defined layers and these will be absent when using shop bought custard. If the custard is homemade, it should be thick, a pint should be enough, depending on the size of the bowl, and there should be enough to cover the sponge completely.

Pour it over the sponge, and in the case of homemade custard, wait for it to set. To avoid a skin on homemade custard cover the surface while warm with cling film.

Whip the cream to soft peak stage, add a drop or two of vanilla extract, a dessertspoon or thereabouts of brandy and a teaspoon of sugar to flavour and sweeten the cream. Pile this decoratively onto the surface of the cold custard having first removed the cling film (it does so interfere with the eating process!). Pull into soft peaks and sprinkle with hundreds and thousands (or grated chocolate or flaked almonds – oh whatever.) Eat & Enjoy.

Bread Pudding (Belly Filler, Bally filler)

The origins of bread pudding go way back, at least as far as the 11th or 12th century, but possibly Bread Pudding is as old as bread itself. Nowadays this is traditionally a sweet pudding made with stale bread and milk but savoury versions also exist, and not just in the Black Country. Mexico, Argentina, Canada and the good old US of A are just a few of the many countries that have their own versions. The humble bread pudding has gone global. Good old-fashioned comfort food.

Modern bread is possibly not the best suited, overly soft and moist, strangled by plastic wrap. Years ago, bread was a different texture, difficult to cut when fresh, maturing overnight, it would be much easier to slice the following day. The pudding was better if the bread was a couple of days old, it dried out as it went stale and although less pleasant to eat for sandwiches, this was perfect for the humble bread pudding.

The idea of the pudding, aside from a tasty treat, was to use up bread that would otherwise go to waste. Sometimes the odd crust would be cut up into small squares and put out for the birds, and if there was any leftover bread pudding, that could be put out too. The suet version would probably be particularly popular with the robins.

There are many alternative recipes, three are included here, the first from Catherine Flavell, who makes "exceedingly good cakes." This is a popular recipe and one of the few based on wholemeal bread. The next is grandmother's recipe, which used to come complete with charcoal currants burnt to the top and the last is an old recipe that uses suet. They all have several things in common, (hardly surprising as they are all bread pudding), spices, better with more than less, fruit which gives added sweetness, and bread mixed to a paste with liquid, either milk or water.

All these variations produce perfectly edible versions with subtle differences, as to the best, try them all – you decide.

1) <u>Catherine Flavell's tried and tested bread pudding, loved by many.</u>

1 wholemeal loaf
As much dried fruit as you want
About 6oz demerara sugar
3 tblsps mixed spice
3 eggs

Put the loaf into a bowl and soak in water – not too much, just enough to mush it up. Add the rest of the ingredients except the butter and mix well. Pour into a greased 9" x 9" tin about 2" deep. Dot the top with knobs of butter. Cook for around an hour at 180°C. If the tops starts to burn cover with a piece of foil.

Devour hot, but expect to burn your mouth or wait until it cools and cut into slabs. The demerara and wholemeal bread add a pleasant depth of flavour and a good colour. If you add cherries and mixed fruit, it is as nice as Christmas pud!

Catherine Flavell's Bread Pudding. Photo: Dorothy Turley, 2016

2. Nanny's Bread Pudding

Remember to sprinkle a few currants on the top before baking for the traditional charcoal topping.

½ a loaf of day old or otherwise stale white bread – but definitely not furry, grandma would frown on fur. The quantity is largely irrelevant, use enough to fill your tin, whichever size will fill the bellies of your hungry.
A good handful of currants
3 tablespoons of sugar, plus more for sprinkling. Golden syrup can be substituted for at least one tablespoon
Heaped teaspoon of mixed spice
Butter
Milk

Same method as for most bread pudding, put the bread into a large jug or bowl and pour in enough milk to soak the bread, but not drown it. Water or half-and-half milk and water could be used instead. Leave for an hour or so until softened and stir in the sugar and dried fruit. Cherries can be added. An adapted pudding was made in our household for years, cherries would be added to the mix, half of this went into a greased tin, before stirring the dried fruit into the remaining half and filling the rest of the tin, to cater for a medium size child who could not abide dried fruit. Years later it transpired she didn't much like cherries either. Children!!

Fill the tin with the mix. Sprinkle more sugar over the top, don't be mean here, it will caramelise slightly during cooking, then sprinkle over the mixed spice and dot the top with nuggets of butter before transferring to a preheated oven around 160/170°C. Check after forty minutes, the top should be browned and if you forgot to tuck the currants that tried to surface for air, under their sodden bread blanket, there should be little lumps of charcoal decorating the surface. Cremate a little longer if necessary. Serve sliced in large slabs when cold, that is if you can resist demolishing straight from the oven.

3. Old Fashioned Bread Pudding

1 white loaf, day old. (This could be a mix of brown, wholemeal, white sliced or crusty – anything will do)
8oz mixed fruit, could also include cherries and a small quantity of chopped glace ginger
3oz suet
Good heaped tablespoon mixed spice
7 tablespoons granulated white sugar plus extra to scatter over the top

Rip the bread into pieces and put it in a large bowl, add just enough water to cover and allow to soak for a few minutes. Squeeze out any excess water, this is not needed. Stir in the mixed fruit, suet, spice and sugar. Mix well with a fork until everything is evenly distributed. Tip into a greased baking tin. Use a deep tin, at least 2" deep and around 9" x 9", there will be quite a lot of mixture.

Place in a preheated oven, 180°C for approximately an hour and a half, check after an hour. The pudding should have browned over the top.

Sprinkle liberally with sugar. The pudding will be puffed and slightly risen when it comes out of the oven, but will soon set into a firm, sliceable slab. Eat hot or cold, with custard or without. None of the quantities are set in stone. If you like more spice – add more, if you don't like mixed fruit, don't use it, add cherries or leave the fruit out completely.

Photo: Angela Parkes, 2016

Bread and Butter Pudding

This is another classic, made from memory rather than recipe and bread that would otherwise go to waste.

"If there was bread and butter left from tea, mum would cover the plate and keep it somewhere cool, the following day it would reappear as a pudding."

Bread pudding is served in solid hunks to grab and go; bread and butter pudding, its lighter cousin is an altogether more refined affair. Served sitting respectably at the table as a proper pudding. It should not be heavy and lumpen; the top should be crisp and golden, the interior layers of soft bread bathed in a just-set custard, studded with fat currants.

8 thin slices of buttered bread
4 dessertspoons of sugar plus more for sprinkling
2oz currants or sultanas – any type of dried fruit
¾ pint of milk
2 eggs
Mixed spice

Grease an ovenproof dish and preheat the oven to about 180°C, 350°F, Gas Mk 4. Cut the bread into quarters, purists would cut off the crusts but there is no harm at all in leaving them on. Overlap a layer in the base of the dish and sprinkle with 2 dessertspoons of sugar then add about half of the currants. Add another layer of bread, 2 more spoons of sugar and the rest of the currants. Top with the last of the bread. Tuck any exposed currants in, as the flavour of burnt currants is not entirely pleasant.

Break two eggs into a jug and add the milk, some of the milk could be replaced with cream, but semi-skimmed milk works almost as well for those counting calories. Beat the eggs and the milk with a fork to combine then pour the mix over the bread. Again proper cooks would probably scald the milk, pour this over the eggs and strain onto the bread, but the easy life beckons. Sprinkle more sugar over the top and add a little mixed spice.

Place into the preheated oven and cook until the top is crisp and golden, the custard below is just set and the smell is enough to make the mouth water, around half an hour.

For those who cannot abide dried fruit, the bread and butter could be spread with jam, turning this into a jam sandwich pudding!

Jam Roly Poly (Shirtsleeve pudding, dead man's arm)

A pudding of immense proportions, nostalgia in a dish, substantial and filling. Traditionally British, and deserving of a regular spot on Black Country tables. A suet based pudding, rolled flat, spread with jam then rolled up like a Swiss roll and steamed. These days it may also be cooked in the oven or microwaved as quicker alternatives. It is served, of course, with custard.

Another name was shirt-sleeve pudding, which related to the cooking method. Once prepared, the pudding was slipped into a shirtsleeve for boiling or steaming, hence one of its other names, dead man's arm. Delicious.

8oz self-raising flour
4oz suet
2oz sugar
Milk to mix
Jam, strawberry or raspberry, anything red!
Pinch of salt

Preheat the oven, 200°C, 180°C fan assisted, Gas Mk 6.

Make the pastry, suet pastry is easy to make and very forgiving. Sift the flour into a bowl, stir in the suet, salt and sugar. Add a couple of tablespoons of milk, water could be used, but given the amount of suet and jam, it would seem churlish to count the calories, not to mention pointless! Keep adding milk until a soft but not sticky dough is formed. Tip onto a floured board and roll to a rectangle approximately 8" x 13". Spread with jam, leaving a jam free border of about half an inch all round. Moisten the edges and roll up like a Swiss roll, starting at the short side.

In the absence of a shirtsleeve, grease a sheet of greaseproof paper, put a pleat in the paper to allow the pudding to expand and place the roly-poly in the middle of the paper. Wrap the pudding loosely in the paper, then wrap loosely in foil. Place a rack over a roasting tin and fill the tin 2/3 full of boiling water. Put the pudding on the rack and place in the preheated oven for about 40 minutes. Serve with custard.

The pudding can be baked without the bain-marie. Once rolled up, place seam side down on a greased baking sheet, sprinkle the top with sugar and bake for 35-40 minutes until golden.

Spotted Dick (Spotted dog, plum bolster)

"Suet pudding made in a bolster case, boiled in a big saucepan. Cut into wedges with hot jam and custard poured over the top. To die for – I can taste it now."

Another classic rib-sticker of a pudding, this time studded with dried fruit. Similar to jam roly-poly this can be flattened into a sheet then rolled up like a Swiss roll with fruit and sugar inside or it can be steamed in a basin. Not overly sweet, the suet pastry does not contain too much sugar; most of the sweetness is derived from the dried fruit and of course, from the essential custard sauce served with it. The pudding can be traced back certainly as far as Victorian times, but it is the name rather than the taste that draws attention, double entendre runs riot. Spotted obviously refers to the appearance given by the currants, but to what does dick refer? There are conflicting theories; the term dick was used to refer to a plain pudding. This is a plain pudding spotted with currants, so it certainly follows that this could be where the name arises. Another theory is this is a corruption of the second part of the word pudding. Puddink to puddick and finally shortened to dick. So many sniggers and connotations have been attached to the name that in some areas it has been banned, renamed Spotted Richard! Spotted dog was a similar pudding but the currants and sugar were stuck in before cooking so they were visible on the outside.

It doesn't really matter how spotted dick got its name it's still a fine nursery pudding, perhaps not invented in the Black Country but certainly eaten there.

8oz self-raising flour
4oz suet
3oz caster sugar
6oz currants
Pinch of salt
Zest of a lemon
Milk

Mix the flour, suet, sugar, salt, lemon zest and currants. Add enough milk to bind, about 6 fl oz, the mixture should be quite soft. Grease a pudding basin, or the pudding will be difficult to turn out and place the mix into the basin. Pleat a sheet of greased foil or greaseproof and cover the top of the basin, tie this in place. Tie a loop over the top of the basin to form a handle. Place the basin into a large saucepan and fill with water until it comes two-thirds up the sides of the basin. Cover with a lid, bring to the boil and boil for half an hour, turn down the heat and simmer for a further hour and a half, make sure the pan does not boil dry. Turn out and serve with custard, lots of custard.

Bananas and Custard

A simple midweek, use what's left pudding, no recipe needed here. A banana was sliced into a desert bowl, a spoonful of sugar sprinkled over the top if there's a sweet tooth otherwise leave it out, bananas are rich in natural sugars. Pour the hot custard over the bananas as soon as they have been sliced or they will discolour, and leave to set. Ready-made custard can be used, and even though the pudding will not set, it will taste almost as good.

Prunes and custard

This is another quick and simple dish remembered from childhood, which again seems to have fallen out of favour. Tinned prunes were used, so it really was as simple as opening a tin. The syrup was thick and sweet and used to sit on top of the custard in a luscious brown layer. As the prunes were eaten, each stone was put on the rim of the dish and counted to the rhyme,

> "Tinker, tailor soldier sailor
> Rich man, poor man, beggar man, thief.
> Silk, satin, cotton, rags.
> This year, next year, sometime, never."

Stewed Fruit

There was often fruit available from the garden; this could have been strawberries in summer, which make a rather nice crumble as does rhubarb, juicy fat green or red gooseberries, plums or apples in the autumn. All of these could be stewed to provide a pie filling or a simple pudding served with custard. The fruit is placed into a pan with a spot of water, a tablespoon or two, just enough to stop the fruit catching on the bottom of the pan. Simmered gently until the fruit is soft; try not to stir too much to preserve the structure of the fruit. Sugar added to taste; some fruit such as rhubarb will take a lot of sugar to become palatable. When the fruit is done, serve hot with custard.

Blackberries

How many people remember blackberrying as a child? Bag or bucket hanging from the wrist, trying to avoid thorns and nettles while reaching for the biggest, juiciest shiny blackberries that were always just out of reach? Purple stains on the fingers, eating more than went home, but it was free food and there were many uses. Apple pie is even better with a handful of blackberries, there is blackberry fool, bramble jelly is a lovely autumn preserve, not to mention blackberry vinegar, blackberry chutney even blackberry port. The downside - well there are two main ones, every blackberry seems to come with its own grub and its takes soooo long to pick enough to make a pot of jam or gallon of wine.

<u>Poached blackberries</u>
A traditional accompaniment to junket, but works equally well with milk jelly or a crumble topping, served with ice cream or custard.

Pick the blackberries, you can buy them in autumn, but somehow this just seems wrong! Soak the fruits in water with a pinch of salt for half an hour; this should get rid of those little white grubs that love the taste of blackberries. You shouldn't need to do this for shop bought berries.

"Mum soaked everything when I was a child, anything likely to harbour grubs was straight into a bowl of water with a generous swoosh of salt, and cauliflower was a firm favourite for the salt treatment."

Drain, then rinse the berries and pop them into a pan, add a little water, just enough to cover and sugar to taste, these are naturally sweet, so shouldn't need too much sugar. When the berries are soft and the cooking liquid deliciously purple remove the berries to a bowl and turn up the heat. Taste and adjust the sugar if need be, and boil to reduce the liquid until it thickens slightly and looks syrupy then add back to the berries. Serve with a shortbread biscuit and ice cream or with a vanilla mousse or junket.

Baked Apples

Simplicity itself, there would often be a glut of apples in the autumn, boxes and bags of them to get through, so fruit puddings feature heavily at this time of year. Baked apples are often overlooked as a pudding; people tend to forget how good the uncomplicated, clean taste can be.

Preheat the oven to 350°F, 175°C. Core one large apple per person with a couple extra, some people don't fully remove the core, only taking out the top half. You could also score a line around the apple at the widest part. Stand these in a baking tin and pack the cavity with a mixture of soft brown sugar, butter and dried fruit. Sprinkle a dusting of cinnamon or mixed spice over the top. Bake for 20 to 30 minutes, may take longer depending on the size of the apples. When these are tender and the flesh starting to "fluff" they are done. Five minutes before these are taken out of the oven dribble a spoonful of golden syrup over the top of the apples. Serve with the caramelised juices from the tin poured over and sweetened whipped cream.

Apple Pie

Another underrated favourite from childhood; soft, cinnamon apple in a crisp pastry shell, served, of course, with custard. There are two versions of thought, do you cook the apples first or do you pile them into the pie raw, so they keep their shape. Both have been tried and both work, apples cook in no time, so by the time the pastry is cooked the apples should also be cooked.

When asked about a favourite pudding, very few people think of apple pie first, but if asked about comfort food or favourite food from childhood then it is a different story, apple pie crops up time and time again. It is even on the menu at McDonald's and a pie that has been about since Chaucer's time must have something going for it! Cooking apples give this a lovely tartness.

Filling
4 large cooking apples or a mix of cooking and dessert.
6oz sugar or to taste, this will be quite sweet
1 teaspoon of cinnamon
Knob of butter

Pastry
12oz plain flour
6oz butter
Pinch of salt
2oz sugar

Preheat the oven 200°C, 400°F, Gas Mark 6. Make the pastry using the method for lemon curd tarts, then place in the fridge to chill.

Peel and core the apples, slice or cut into small chunks. Put the apples in a pan with a knob of butter and a tablespoon of water. Heat gently for a few minutes, stirring only occasionally so they do not break up too much. They will soon begin to soften and release juices, stir in the sugar a little at a time, tasting as you go until it is sweet enough and most of the apples are still unbroken. Take the apples off the heat and mix in the cinnamon.

Cut the pastry in half and roll one-half out, use this to line a pie dish, prick the base with a fork and pile the filling in. You could bake the base blind for a few minutes to ensure you do not fall victim to the now infamous soggy bottom before putting the filling in. Roll out the rest of the pastry to form the lid. Place this over the apples, trim off the excess and crimp the edges. Brush the top with milk and bake for around 30 minutes until the pastry is golden and crisp. Remove from the oven and sprinkle the top with caster sugar. Serve with custard, cream or ice cream.

Apple Crumble

Another classic British pudding, nothing special but the crumble topping is comfort in a bowl. Children often love the sweet crumbly topping, particularly when served with custard. So although this dish is heavy in sugar and fat when made the traditional way, it is a good way of getting fruit into children. There are ways of making the topping more healthy, by adding oats to the crumble and cutting back on fat. But there is no denying, the old-fashioned recipe still tastes good.

Crumble topping
10oz plain flour
6oz butter
6oz sugar
Pinch of salt

Filling
1lb apples
3 tablespoons sugar or to taste
Knob of butter

½ tsp cinnamon

Preheat the oven to 180°C, 160°C fan assisted oven, 350°F, Gas Mark 4. Peel the apples and cut into a saucepan with a splash of water and a knob of butter, stir over a medium heat until the apples begin to break down, stir in the sugar and adjust to taste. Add the cinnamon and transfer to a heatproof bowl.

Next, make the crumble. Stir the flour, salt and sugar together, rub in the butter until the mixture resembles fine breadcrumbs. Sprinkle the topping over the fruit and cook for 25 – 30 minutes until the topping is lightly browned, serve with custard, cream, ice cream or all of these. Some people prefer the fruit to look like fruit; this can be sliced straight into the heatproof bowl. Sprinkle the sugar and cinnamon over the top then add the topping and bake for a little longer until the fruit is tender. In the autumn, blackberries make a tasty addition to the filling.

Rhubarb crumble

Yet another fruit based classic, prepare exactly as above but the rhubarb will need more sugar. When cooking the rhubarb in the pan, try not to stir too much or the rhubarb will break down into rhubarb mush instead of chunks, but it will still taste as good. Leave out the cinnamon, but a little finely chopped stem ginger, just one or two pieces from a jar could be added to the fruit along with a spoon or two of the syrup.

Apple turnover

Any leftover apple or pastry can be worked into an apple turnover to provide another pudding. The pastry is rolled out into a sheet and the fruit piled up on one-half, leaving a border all around. The edges of the pastry are moistened with milk, the pastry is then folded over the filling to form a pocket, and the edges pressed to seal them.

Bake in a preheated oven at 180°C for around 20 to 25 minutes until the pastry is crisp and golden. Serve with custard.

Jam Turnover

Leftover pastry can be filled with jam, instead of apple as in the above recipe and cooked in the same way.

Treacle Tart

Another traditional favourite that uses up leftover bread, although a more appropriate name would be golden syrup tart. Treacle is too strongly flavoured.

Pastry – see apple pie recipe

12oz golden syrup
4 tablespoons soft white breadcrumbs
2 tablespoons lemon juice and a little zest if liked.

Preheat the oven 190°C, 375°F or Gas Mark 5. Roll the pastry out and line a flan dish, bake blind for 10 to 15 minutes. Mix together filling ingredients and fill the pastry case. If this is too runny, add more breadcrumbs. A pinch of ginger also works well with the syrup. The lemon juice takes the edge off the sweetness but could be left out. Bake for around 30 minutes. Serve with cream or custard.

Sweet sultana dumplings

Mini steamed puddings by another name.

4oz breadcrumbs
4oz plain flour
4oz sultanas
2oz sugar

1 egg
Pinch salt
Milk to mix.

Mix all the ingredients to a soft dough, break off bits and roll into dumplings. Place in a steamer over boiling water and steam for ten minutes and serve.

Treacle Pudding

This is a very old recipe that uses no eggs, it has not been tested, instead of steaming for hours, most steamed puddings will microwave in 5 minutes.

1 cup self-raising flour
2 tablespoons of sugar
2 tablespoons butter or dripping
2 tablespoons treacle
Pinch salt
1 teaspoon ginger
1 cup of milk

Mix the dry ingredients, rub in the butter. Add the treacle and the milk and mix. Steam in a buttered mould for at least 2 hours. Serve with custard.

Slow Cooker Syrup Sponge

The light, moist syrup sponge of youth can easily be made in a slow cooker.

4oz self-raising flour
4oz butter
4oz sugar brown or white
2 eggs

Golden syrup

Cream the butter and sugar, beat in the eggs then sift in the flour. Grease a pudding basin and pour at least an inch of syrup into the bottom, then add the sponge mixture. Cover with a piece of pleated, greased foil and place in a slow cooker. Add enough water to come halfway up the sides of the dish and cook on high for 3½ to 4 hours until cooked through, light and moist. Turn out and serve with custard.

Marmalade Pudding

A way of using up half pots of marmalade and day old bread. Instead of an orange cap, the marmalade is stirred through the mix, so every bite is full of sticky, tangy flavour. Whisky works well with orange, a tablespoon or two could be added to the mix to give extra flavour. The marmalade needs to be mixable here, not too thick, if it has set too well in the jar, thin it with a spot of boiling water – not too thin it should still have some body

12oz marmalade
2 large eggs, separated, and 2 egg yolks
8fl oz cream
4oz caster sugar
6oz white breadcrumbs

Preheat the oven 180°C, 160°C fan assisted, Gas Mk 4 and grease an ovenproof dish. Mix the marmalade with all the egg yolks, the cream, and the caster sugar, beat well until completely blended, stir in all but a heaped tablespoon of the breadcrumbs. Whisk the egg whites to soft peak stage and fold these into the marmalade mixture. Transfer to the ovenproof dish, stand this in a baking tin, pour in boiling water until it comes halfway up the sides of the dish, and sprinkle the last of the crumbs over the top of the pudding. Cook 50-60 minutes until just set but not solid.

Marmalade pudding (II)

This is so good, one recipe is not enough. Not often made nowadays it was one pudding that came up in a list of most popular puds in the Black Country for the book.

6oz fine brown breadcrumbs
5oz soft brown sugar
1oz self-raising wholemeal flour (white at a push)
6oz butter
8 tablespoons marmalade
3 eggs
1 tsp bicarbonate of soda

Grease a 3-pint heatproof basin. Mix the flour, sugar and breadcrumbs, melt the butter with the marmalade and pour into the dry ingredients, mix well. Beat the eggs until frothy and beat into the pudding mix. Dissolve the bicarb in a tablespoon of water and add this to the pudding before transferring it to the greased basin. Cover with a tight fitting, pleated greaseproof or greased foil lid and steam for 2 hours.

Lemon Surprise Pudding (Saucy Lemon Pud, Self-Saucing Lemon Pudding)

"Children love magic and it always seemed like magic when mum took a golden brown sponge pudding out of the oven, as the spoon lifted out the first serving, underneath was a pool of lemon sauce the pudding had made all by itself while it was in the oven. Magic."

A tangy, lemon pudding that separates as it cooks; in the bottom of the dish is a custardy/lemon curd like sauce topped by a soft sponge.

2oz/50g butter
8oz/200g sugar

4fl oz/100 ml lemon juice plus zest of 1 lemon
3 eggs
2oz/50g plain flour
8fl oz/250ml milk
Few drops vanilla essence

Preheat the oven 180°C, 160°C fan assisted, Gas Mark 4. Put butter, sugar and lemon zest in a bowl and cream until light and fluffy. Separate the eggs. Add the lemon juice, egg yolks, flour, milk and vanilla to the creamed mixture, mix well after each addition. Whisk the egg whites until stiff but not dry and fold into the cake mixture. Pour into a greased ovenproof dish and stand this in a baking tin half filled with water. Cook for 40-45 minutes until the top is golden brown and risen and there is a sauce in the bottom of the bowl.

Pineapple upside down pudding

A blast from the past with another retro pudding. Children, in particular, loved the look of the pineapple and cherries on the top. Adding golden syrup gives a lovely mellow flavour, but it will work just as well if you leave this out.

<u>Cake</u>
4oz butter
4oz self-raising flour
4oz sugar
1 egg

<u>Topping</u>
3 tablespoons golden syrup or 2oz brown sugar mixed with 2oz butter
1 tin pineapple
Glace cherries

Preheat the oven to 180°C, 160°C fan assisted, Gas Mark 4. Grease a round cake tin and if using syrup, spoon this into the bottom of the tin and arrange whole rings of pineapple in the base of the tin. If sugar and butter mix is being used for the topping, spread this over the base of the tin and a little way up the sides – as far as the fruit is likely to come up, and then add the pineapple. Put a glace cherry in the hole in the middle of each ring and fill up any spaces with bits of pineapple and cherries.

Cream the butter and sugar for the cake mix, beat in the egg and a tablespoon of the syrup from the pineapple. Fold in the flour, if it seems a little dry add a spot of milk, then pour the mix over the pineapple in the tin. Level the top and bake for around 35 minutes until golden brown. Remove from the tin and allow to stand for five minutes. Run a palate knife down the sides all the way round to loosen. Put a plate over the top, close your eyes, hold your breath, invert the plate and hope the pineapple is attached to the cake, not the tin when you open your eyes. Serve warm with ice cream, custard, or a pineapple sauce made with a tablespoon of cornflour, the rest of the syrup from the tin and pineapple juice.

Apple Snow

Another ancient dish dating back to the Elizabethan era. A busy mum's dream of a pudding, simple to prepare and few ingredients to source, no wonder it was so popular in using up all those apples. There was often a bowl of this lurking in the fridge for pudding, but it would evaporate through the day, as little spoons tested the mousse like mix at very regular intervals. Dessert apples are good in this, not cheek suckingly sour like cookers.

8 apples
4oz sugar
2 egg whites
4 fl oz double cream or a small pot, quantities are not critical here

1 tsp cinnamon (optional)
Juice and peel of 1 lemon (optional)

Peel, core and chop the apples, place these in a pan with the lemon juice and/or cinnamon if using. Add 2oz sugar and heat gently, stirring now and then until the apples are very soft. Taste and add more sugar if needed. Allow to cool, then refrigerate until cold. Beat the apples until a smooth puree is obtained. Whip the cream to soft peak stage and whisk the egg whites to stiff peak stage, fold a little of the remaining sugar into the egg whites. Fold the cream and the egg whites into the stewed apple and refrigerate until needed.

This is also lovely with some stewed rhubarb or stewed blackberries folded through after the cream and egg whites have been added, to leave pinkish, flavour packed trails in the snow.

You could replace the apples with rhubarb to make rhubarb snow.

Gooseberry fool

Gooseberries seem to have fallen out of favour now; perhaps it was finding children under the gooseberry bush that did it. Many Black Country houses had one of these bushes in the back garden. The fruits were green or red, but always hairy. A fool, at least the culinary version, is a pudding made by folding fruit puree through custard. These days, the custard may be replaced by whipped cream or even yoghurt. Another British classic and judging by the number of gooseberry bushes, a Black Country classic too. Use sharp fruits to contrast with the sweet custard.

Puree
1lb gooseberries
4oz Sugar

Custard

½ pint milk
1 tsp cornflour
1 egg, beaten plus one egg yolk
Few drops of vanilla essence
2 tablespoons of sugar

Make the custard: Scald the milk with the sugar and vanilla essence, heat to boiling point, cool slightly. Put the eggs in a bowl and beat to combine, mix to a smooth paste with the cornflour, pour in the milk a little at a time, mixing until all the milk is incorporated, then return to the pan and heat gently, stirring constantly until the custard thickens. The mixture will catch easily so keep stirring. Strain the mix and refrigerate until cool. For a good fool, everything should be cool.

Top and tail the gooseberries and put them in a pan with the sugar and a little water. Simmer gently until they are very tender, you could add the juice of a lemon. Then sieve the gooseberries to remove the hairs and give a smooth puree. Chill.

Stir the gooseberries through the custard.

You could also whip half a pint of cream and fold this through to lighten the mixture. Another version also incorporates stiffly whisked egg whites. Everything needs to be cold then folded together.

In an early recipe this was served semifreddo, i.e. part frozen, this can be achieved by putting the fool in a metal bowl inside a container filled with ice and salt, this acts like a modern ice cream maker, alternatively place in the freezer, but do not freeze solid, just leave it until the fool begins to freeze.

Junket

Another blast from the past, this custardy pudding has been with us since medieval times. I remember it from childhood when mum used to make it, but I haven't seen rennet on sale for a long time now. A milk based pudding that is set to a soft, sweet custard using rennet. Rennet is a digestive enzyme found in the fourth stomach of calves, which coagulates milk. Starting to go off your milk pudding yet? There are vegetarian options available for making cheese, but as it became more difficult to get hold of, junket dropped out of fashion. For those of you who may still be able to source the magic ingredient that curdles your milk, the recipe is below. Can't vouch for this, it's an old recipe from mums cookbook that I have never tried to make. You can add flavour at will, rosewater to mirror the medieval folks, good old vanilla (there's nothing wrong with vanilla – have you never read Fifty Shades of Grey?), fruit or coffee, the choice is yours. The recipe should serve four.

1 pint milk
2 tablespoons sugar
2 teaspoons rennet
½ teaspoon (or to taste) vanilla essence
Nutmeg

Warm the milk, sugar and vanilla gently until it is about blood heat, it will feel lukewarm to the touch, between 90 – 110°F but it must not be too hot or it will denature the rennet meaning it won't work. Add the rennet, stir for a few seconds only, before removing from the heat and dividing the pudding between four dishes, or alternatively, you could set this in a pint dish. Grate a little nutmeg over the top and leave to set in a cool place undisturbed for around two hours. Once the junket is cut, the curd will separate from the whey, which will run out as a clear liquid.

Chocolate Concrete (Chocolate Crunch)

Now, I was in two minds about this. Is it really a Black County dish? And what is Chocolate Concrete anyway? Some people remember school dinners fondly, others not so much but this seems to be one dish from their school days that unites people, they liked it! Additionally, it does appear to be something regularly prepared in Black Country school kitchens to this day but few outside the region (that will admit to it anyway). A chocolatey shortcake so hard when attacked with a spoon, it would fly out of the bowl and bounce off the opposite wall, that is if it didn't bend the spoon first. Not even dented, this could be picked up, dusted off and carry on where it left the plate!

Chocolate concrete was not confined to schools, once served at RAF Cosford where it was known to stave off hunger pains; it coped well with being stored in the pocket until consumption, ideal with a mug of hot sweet tea outside on a winter's day with a freezing wind howling down the runway.

So here it is, the stuff of childhood, straight from the 1970's, chocolate concrete and do not forget the pink custard to serve with it.

5 ½ lbs self-raising flour
4 ½ lbs butter
4 ½ lbs sugar
8oz cocoa powder
8 eggs

Mix the dry ingredients while you gently melt the butter. Pour this onto the dry ingredients and add the eggs one at a time. Place in a preheated oven (170°C) for 45 minutes or thereabouts. Serves 120.

Not that hungry? Try the recipe below

8oz plain flour
2oz cocoa or drinking chocolate
4oz sugar
4oz melted butter

Mix the dry ingredients, stir in the melted butter. Transfer to a greased 7" baking tin and cook at Mk 3 or 160°C for around 45 minutes until concrete like!! Serve with pink custard.

School puddings were accompanied by an eclectic collection of sauces including molten red jam of indeterminate origin and custard in a variety of hues, brown (chocolate), bright green (mint), pink (strawberry) and good old fashioned yellow.

Pink Custard (Blancmange by another name!!)

1 pint milk
1 strawberry blancmange powder
2 to 3 heaped tablespoons sugar

In a jug mix the blancmange powder and sugar, add two tablespoons of cold milk and mix to a paste. Put the milk on to scald in a pan, do not boil. Pour the hot milk over the blancmange paste, mix and then transfer the whole lot to a saucepan. Heat, stirring all the time until it thickens to the desired consistency. Serve. If you allow it to go cold this will set into another gloriously old-fashioned pudding.

Mint Custard (Puke custard)

Same technique as above but use vanilla blancmange with a drop of green colour and a few drops of peppermint extract. For the non-purists, ready-made custard with a drop of green colour and a few drops of peppermint essence will produce and interesting lime green result.

Lemon curd tarts

At Christmas, as an alternative to mince pies and another fond memory from childhood. Lemon curd is easy to make, but Edna May's lemon curd was the product of choice, tart and lemony, just perfect with sweet shortcrust pastry.

<u>Sweet shortcrust pastry</u>
3oz butter
6oz plain flour
1oz sugar (you could use icing sugar or caster sugar)

<u>Filling</u>
Edna May Lemon Curd, or any other premium brand

To make the pastry, using your fingertips rub the butter into the flour until it resembles fine breadcrumbs. Stir in the sugar. Keep everything as cold as possible while you are working, it will help keep the pastry short. Bring the pastry together into a ball; if this is too dry add some cold water a spoonful at a time. Roll the pastry out on a floured board to around ¼" thick. Using a 3" cutter, cut 12 rounds and place in a greased tartlet tray. Add a teaspoon of lemon curd to each, don't overfill or the lemon curd will bubble out and caramelise on the tin, it will weld the pastry to the metal and you'll lose some of the filling. (If this does happen, run a knife around the edge of the pastry while the curd is still hot.) Bake at 200°C or 180°C in a fan oven for 12-15 minutes, until the pastry is just starting to colour.

<u>Jam Tarts</u>
Made in exactly the same way as lemon curd tarts, but using jam to fill. More of an everyday fare and perfect for using up that extra bit of jam from a batch that wouldn't fill a whole jar.

Fruit salad

This was another special tea recipe, as I remember, served in a shallow fruit dish in its own syrup, with a little carnation milk poured over the top.

Apples
Strawberries
Grapes
Banana
Pears
Sugar to taste
Lemon – juice only

This can be made with any combination of fruit, use whatever is to hand. Peel and chop the flesh from the apples and pears into small (but not too small) pieces and put these in a serving bowl. Add the lemon juice and mix to prevent the fruit browning. Hull the strawberries and slice these in along with the grapes, make sure any stalks are removed. Peel and slice in the banana and mix. Lemon juice was not always used, but this will prevent the apple and banana discolouring. Add a couple of tablespoons of sugar and mix through. Cover the bowl and leave somewhere cool for a couple of hours. A syrup will form around the fruit. Taste for sweetness and add more sugar if required. If the sugar is added as soon as the fruit is in the bowl and stirred in, there should be little discolouration of any of the fruit.

Pikelets

These don't have their roots firmly in the Black Country, the name itself is derived from the Welsh, Bara Pyglyd (pitchy bread), but they are a regional bread that has been adopted by the people.

Locally known as pikelets, this does seem to be a term more commonly found in the Midlands than elsewhere. Springy, round creations full of holes and about half an inch thick. Pikelets were not perfectly round, they were freeform, poor man's crumpets for those who did not have the metal ring to provide shape and give extra depth. Batter was dropped into the pan or onto the hot griddle to find its own shape; these would spread thinner than crumpets.

Many will remember toasting them at arm's length over the glow of an open fire, then eating laden with enough butter to run through the holes, down the fingers and chin, leaving greasy tell-tail signs on a clean shirt.

"Catherine Flavell: My Husbands Grandmother was a widow in the 1920s. She used to make Pikelets and his Dad had to take them around and sell them in Hurst Hill."

They can be tricky to get right, if the batter is too thick enough holes will not form. There can be problems setting the batter all the way through. In one attempt, the taste left a little to be desired, yeasty and slightly fermented but the main problem was semi-raw batter in the middle, no matter how long it was cooked. The batter rose well, the holes were just about perfect but as for the texture and the taste – no so much.

8oz flour
1 x 7g sachet yeast
1 teaspoon sugar
10 fluid ounces milk and water mixed, warmed to blood heat
1 teaspoon of salt
½ teaspoon bicarbonate of soda

2oz extra flour for pikelets – but check thickness of batter before adding it all

Stir the sugar and yeast into the warm liquid, do not over warm this, if the temperature is too high it will kill the yeast and the mixture

will not rise. Put the flour into a bowl and stir in the liquid, beat well to a smooth batter, cover with cling film and leave in a warm place to rise for about an hour to an hour and a half, this will take longer if the room is cool. The mixture will increase in size, bubbles will form on the surface and the cling film will bow as the yeast respires and pressure increases. After a while, the mixture may begin to fall back a little, don't worry if it doesn't.

Mix the salt, bicarbonate of soda and 1 tablespoon of boiling water. Stir into the pikelet mixture. The batter should be pourable, but thickish, about the consistency of double cream for crumpets, slightly thicker for pikelets. Add more water if necessary to thin it down a little.

Rest the batter for another 15 minutes. If making crumpets, grease the inside of the metal rings, straight sided pastry cutters will work for this, also grease a griddle or heavy bottom frying pan. Do not over heat, aim for low to medium heat or the bottom of the pikelets will burn before they are cooked. For pikelets drop spoonfuls of batter onto the griddle, for crumpets two-thirds fill the rings. If the batter leaks out from the rings it is too thin, add another tablespoon

of flour to the mix. Once on the heat, leave well alone until bubbles rise to the surface and the surface is set. You may need to help the bubbles by pricking some with a fork. If there are very few bubbles, the mixture may be too thick, add a little more liquid and try again. If there is not much experience of pikelet making, it is generally better to sacrifice the first one as a tester to ensure the thickness of the batter and the heat on the griddle are suitable.

After 4-5 minutes, the crumpets/pikelets should be done, flip them over and cook the other side for another couple of minutes.

Serve while hot with far too much butter and jam, or allow to cool and toast to reheat later. They will keep for a couple of days in a polythene bag.

Cake 'ole

An empty cake tin, oh the shame. A cup of tea and a slice of cake always waited for visitors, at least the welcome ones. Cake should be in the tin at all times, cake in abundance and an abundance of recipes to bake. The earliest memories of cooking are often of standing on a stool in grandma's kitchen, stirring a cake batter or making rock cakes. Cooking is a form of time travel, skills and recipes spanning generations, the taste of those cakes in later years transports us straight back to nanny's kitchen.

Rock Cakes

"There's no going wrong with a rock cake. The rough finish on these buns reminds me of dolloping spoonful's of mix onto a baking tray to cook so many years ago now, I must have been around three years old, but still remember the cool, dark kitchen and floury apron as we worked. Nana lives on in her rock cakes!"

8oz self-raising flour
1 teaspoon of baking power
3oz caster sugar
4oz butter
4oz currants
1 egg
Milk to mix

Sift the flour and baking powder into a bowl. Stir in the sugar. Add the butter and cut in with a sharp knife, then rub the mixture with the fingertips until it resembles fine breadcrumbs. Add the currants and stir well to distribute these. Beat the egg and the milk together and use this to bind the breadcrumb mixture to a firm dough. Place spoonfuls onto a greased baking sheet leaving plenty of room between as these will flatten and spread a little as they cook. Bake for 15 – 20 minutes in a preheated oven (350°F, 180°C, Gas Mk 4). They should be firm on top and golden when done, cool for a couple of minutes on the tin, then transfer to a wire rack. They will firm up more as they cool. You could add any mixed/dried fruit, cherries for example or blueberries, even chocolate chips or fudge pieces, substitute brown sugar for white, add cinnamon and brown sugar, nutmeg or mixed spice. These are nice served warm from the oven, dredged with caster sugar and buttered.

Raspberry drops (Raspberry buns)

A mother-in-law special, and sadly her recipe passed with her, which was a great loss. These flat, semi-crunchy buns with their red jam centres piled up in the cake tin will always remind me of moments that cannot be recaptured in a mix of cake, scone and cookie.

3oz butter
3oz sugar
Few drops of vanilla essence
1 egg
8oz self-raising flour
Raspberry jam

Preheat the oven to 180°C, Gas Mark 4. Cream the butter and sugar until light and fluffy, add the vanilla essence. Beat in the egg, then sift in the flour and combine. The mixture should be stiff enough to roll but if it seems too dry add a little milk. Roll teaspoonful's into balls and place on a greased baking sheet, allow plenty of room between, make a small dip in the top of each and fill this with half a teaspoon of jam. Bake for 15 minutes until golden. Cool on the tray.

Caramel Rum Rice pudding cake

"I confess, I thought I had never heard of this. Rice pudding cake, is it a pudding or is it a cake? But researching recipes brought back memories of Dad telling me about the rice pudding of his childhood, "sometimes it would be baked longer," he'd said, "we'd have it in slices." I wonder now if this is what he meant."

This recipe puts a more modern spin on rice pudding cake, it still can't decide whether it is a pudding or a cake, but delicious nevertheless.

Caramel
½ cup granulated white sugar.
¼ cup of water

Pudding
½ cup of brown sugar
4 cups of milk – you can also use single cream, condensed milk or a mixture
2/3 cup of pudding rice
2 eggs
Vanilla essence
2 tablespoons rum
2oz raisins

Soak the raisins in the rum. Preheat the oven to 350°F, grease an 8" cake tin. Make a caramel by dissolving the white sugar and water in a small pan, stir occasionally, and brush any stray sugar crystals down the side of the pan with a wet pastry brush until they have all dissolved. When you are sure all the sugar has dissolved, turn up the heat and boil without stirring until the caramel turns a rich golden colour. Once it begins to change colour, this can happen quite quickly, so take care not to burn the caramel. Pour this into the cake tin and coat the bottom of the tin with the caramel.

Make a rice pudding by putting the sugar, milk and rice into a pan, bring to the boil, stirring, turn down the heat and cook until most of the milk has been absorbed, continue to stir or the mix may catch. Take off the heat and cool for a few minutes, stir occasionally to prevent the mixture from forming lumps or setting on the bottom of the pan. Stir in the rum and the raisins. Beat the eggs with the vanilla and add to the pudding. Transfer to the tin and cook for around three-quarters of an hour until the top is browned but the cake is not quite set in the middle. Turn out and serve cut into slices with cream.

Rice Pudding Cake Old Black Country Style

4oz ground rice
4oz suet
4oz self-raising flour
4oz sugar
1 cup of milk
Pinch salt
1 teaspoon mixed spice

Mix the rice, suet, flour, sugar, salt and spice. Add the milk and mix, transfer to a greased enamel pie dish or basin. Cover with foil and stream for about three hours. A solid pudding!

Lardy Cake (lardy bread, lardy Johns, dough cake, fourses cake)

Lardy Cake did not originate in the Midlands but has long been a favourite here. Found in many areas where pig production is common and that certainly ties in with the Black Country. Wiltshire is the most likely point of origin but the cake has ancient roots, which can be traced back to the fourteen hundreds, giving it plenty of time to spread to the Midlands. Commercially produced Lardy cake has a tendency to be hard and dry, proper stuff is moist, rich and moreish but not greasy, richly caramelised where the sugar has seeped out, melting on the pan leaving a sticky coating that once tasted is likely to be remembered. Not a cake for the faint-hearted, of those of faint heart who should take evasive action at the merest hint of cholesterol.

In all honesty, unless you're making bread which forms the basis for this, it's a bit of a faff, probably not something to make every weekend. Firstly because of the sugar and fat content, which combined can make up more than the weight of the rest of the ingredients; secondly because of the effort. There is yeast in the mix too, so alongside the time taken to layer the lard, as you would in a Danish pastry or puff pastry, there is additional proving time.

The name "fourses" was the afternoon equivalent of "elevenses," the cake was eaten as part of afternoon tea or just with a cuppa to get you through an afternoon's work.

1lb strong white flour
½oz lard for the bread dough
Pinch of salt
2 x 7g sachets of yeast
10fl oz water
6oz lard
6oz currants
6oz sugar

Make the bread dough by mixing the flour, salt and yeast together. Rub in the lard. Add most of the water and using your hands mix the dough, if you need to; add the rest of the water. The dough should be soft, but firm enough to knead. Scatter a little flour on the worktop and knead the dough for 5-10 minutes until it is smooth. Put this back into a clean bowl, cover with a tea towel and leave to rise in a warm place until the dough has doubled in size (1 -2 hours). Tip the dough onto a floured surface and roll it into a rectangle about ¼" thick. Soften the lard so that it is spreadable and cover the dough with the 1/3 of the lard, scatter over 1/3 of the currants and 1/3 of the sugar. Fold the top and bottom in towards the middle and turn the dough a quarter turn. Roll out again and spread with the second 1/3 of the lard, scatter with another 1/3 currants and sugar, then repeat this so all the lard, currants and sugar are used. Grease a baking tin or tray around 8" x 12" and roll the dough out so that it will fit in the tin. Score the cake into squares and cover, put aside for a further 30 minutes or so until risen, then brush the top with melted lard. Bake in a preheated oven 200°C, 180°C (fan assisted), Gas Mark 6 for around 30 – 35 minutes, until golden and cooked through. Cool for a few minutes in the tin, and then transfer to a wire rack. Eat warm, cold, with butter, without. Oh, just eat it and be done.

Dripping Cake (Drippers)

A variation on Lardy Cake, which as the name suggests uses dripping as the fat source. Traditionally, this would have been the dripping left over from a roast joint of meat. Rich with dried fruit, sugar and spice, the dripping would form a sweet thick layer on the bottom of the cake. Wonderful.

The recipe is the same as above, but use dripping, not the brown jelly, just the fat. You may be able to find paper wrapped blocks of beef dripping, similar to lard, but more difficult to obtain these days.

Fruit cake

Every Black Country household had a fruitcake recipe, often slightly different but all variations on the same theme.

6oz/150g butter
6oz/150g sugar
6oz/150g mixed fruit. This can include raisins, currants, sultanas, glace cherries and/or candid peel
12oz/300g self-raising flour
Pinch salt
3 eggs
1 tsp mixed spice
1 cup cold tea

Soak the dried fruit in the cold tea for one hour. Grease and line an 8" cake tin. Preheat the oven to 170°C. Drain the fruit. Combine all the ingredients, transfer to the tin and bake for about 1 ½ hours, test with a skewer to see if it's done, if the skewer comes out clean the cake is cooked.

Butterfly cakes

A staple of the cake tin, quickly and easily made, ideal with a cup of tea. Traditional cakes tended to be loaves or larger round cakes, individual servings were unusual. These are more refined, afternoon tea for ladies who lunch rather than plain tea in the afternoon.

4oz butter
4oz sugar
4oz self-raising flour
1 egg

Buttercream
5oz butter
10oz icing sugar

Jam

Cream the butter and the sugar until light and fluffy. Flavouring could be added, vanilla essence or coffee, beat the egg then beat this into the butter and sugar, if it shows signs of curdling add a tablespoon of the flour to stabilise. Then sift in the rest of the flour and fold into the mix. Divide between cake cases and bake in a preheated oven 180°C fan assisted oven, 200°C or Gas Mark 6 for 15 minutes until golden and springy. Cool on a wire rack. While cooling make the buttercream. Sift the icing sugar into a bowl and cream in the butter, add flavour if desired. When cold cut an inverted cone into the top of the cake. Cut the piece you have taken out of the cake in half, so it can be reattached as "Butterfly wings." Fill the hollow in the cake with a little jam in the bottom, then a dollop of buttercream. Reattach the wings to give you a butterfly cake.

Seed Cake (Caraway Cake, Caraway Seed Cake)

"Father had two aunties, who he visited regularly, generally of a weekend when he was expected to stay to tea. There was, as with all Black Country teas, cake. Father was born in 1923, so this would probably have been in the early '30's, before WWII when he was still quite young, the visits may well have continued into the 1950's. The aunties were skilled bakers with several specialities, Cherry cake, which he loved up until he died, Madeira cake, served buttered, which was another favourite, fruitcake was acceptable. But seed cake, peppered with caraway seeds, a firm favourite with the aunties, he hated. He hated it when he was young, and even more when he was older. The seeds get stuck under my

plate, he would complain. When he left following tea, the cake would as often as not leave with him, hidden in his pocket."

Cheaper than dried fruit which no doubt increased their use, caraway seeds have a strong flavour, reminiscent of lemony aniseed and the secret of a successful cake is how few seeds you add, not how many. Perhaps the aunties were not familiar with this particular cooking tip. Maybe they contributed to the fact that Seed Cake has fallen out of favour and is rarely seen these days. Just saying…

6oz self-raising flour
6oz butter
6oz sugar
2 eggs
1 tsp caraway seeds
2oz ground almonds
4 tablespoons of milk

Preheat the oven to 160°C. Cream the butter and the sugar until light and fluffy. Beat in the eggs one at a time. Stir in the almonds and the caraway seeds, and then sift in the flour. Fold this into the mixture; add enough milk to give a soft dropping consistency. Turn into a greased loaf tin. Level the top and bake for about an hour. It should be well risen, golden and spring back when the top is pressed. Listen to your cake! If it is not singing – it is cooked.

Pound cake

Pound cakes were so called because they used a pound of each of the four key ingredients, flour, butter, sugar and eggs. By today's standards that would produce a far larger cake than most of us would need so this recipe has been scaled down but kept to the same ratio. Not all had fruit in; you could leave this out of you wanted to or substitute cherries or blueberries

8oz self-raising flour
8oz sugar
8oz butter

4 large eggs
8oz currants
8oz sultanas

Preheat the oven to 160°C, grease and line and 8" cake tin. Mix all the ingredients together and transfer to the tin. Level the surface and bake for about an hour and a quarter or until a skewer comes out clean.

Madeira cake

Made to the same recipe as above, but without the fruit. The grated zest of a lemon could be added, 2 tablespoons of golden syrup also works. Wonderful for tea served sliced and buttered.

Date and walnut cake

Sticky, dense, moist and popular, beloved of generations past. Tastes good, keeps well and freezes well. What more could you ask from a cake? You can buy those cooking packs of dry, tasteless dates or one of date shaped boxes, filled with tiny, tough little fruit and a peculiarly shaped plastic fork that you find lingering in the pantry after Easter, where they have been languishing left over from Christmas, possibly not the last Christmas either. But if you want a serious cake, one you want to cut and come again, invest in Medjool dates. Proper dates that yield under the fingers, soft, sticky, luscious dates that people actually enjoy eating.

8oz dates.
1 mug of hot tea (builders, no milk or sugar)
1 teaspoon of bicarbonate of soda
Pinch salt
10oz self-raising flour
4oz butter
5oz dark soft brown sugar

1 tablespoon golden syrup or treacle, treacle will add to the dark brown colour
2oz walnuts, shelled and chopped
1 beaten egg

Stone the dates and chop these finely, put into a bowl with the bicarb and the salt. Add the hot tea and leave to soak, overnight if there is time but for at least an hour. If Medjool dates are used they should be soft and sticky to begin with so won't need as long to soak as other types.

Preheat the oven to 180°C, 160°C for a fan-assisted oven, Gas Mark 4. Sift the flour into a mixing bowl, rub in the butter until this looks like fine breadcrumbs, stir in the sugar and the walnuts. Tip in the dates and the soaking liquid together with the beaten egg and syrup or treacle, combine all the ingredients and put into a greased 2lb loaf tin, bake for around 45 minutes until a skewer comes out clean. This will keep for about a week in a tin. Serve sliced and buttered.

Marmalade Cake

Marmalade was a commonly prepared preserve in the winter months, often there would be part of a batch left over that did not quite fill a jar, this was a way of using up this leftover marmalade.

8oz self-raising flour
Pinch of salt
4oz butter
4oz caster sugar
1 teaspoon orange rind, finely grated (optional)
2 eggs, beaten together
2 tablespoons orange marmalade
2 tablespoons milk

Sift the flour and salt into a large bowl and rub in the butter until the mixture resembles fine breadcrumbs. Stir in the sugar, the orange rind and then add the eggs, marmalade and the milk, the mixture should resemble a thick batter. Pour into a greased tin and bake in the centre of a pre-heated oven at 350°F, 175°C, Gas Mark 4 for around an hour and a quarter until golden brown and a skewer comes out clean. Cool on a wire rack.

Date slices

A cross between a flapjack and date and walnut cake.

6oz dates – see comments for date and walnut
1 cup of hot tea (about 4fl oz)
6oz plain flour
4oz light brown sugar
Pinch of salt
4oz porridge oats
5oz butter

Preheat the oven to 200°C, 180°C Fan assisted, Gas Mark 6. Grease and line an 8-inch square tin. Remove the stones from the dates and chop finely, transfer to a bowl and pour over the hot tea. Put the flour, sugar, oats and salt in a large mixing bowl and stir to mix, rub in the butter to make a crumble. Place half the crumble mix in the bottom of the baking tin, drain the dates and place these on top of the crumble mix, then top with the rest of the crumble mix. Press down lightly, not too hard, or the crumble effect will be lost. Bake for 35 minutes until golden.

Viennese Whirls

So short they melt in the mouth, always a firm favourite, eat your heart out Mr Kipling.

3oz butter
1oz icing sugar
½ tsp vanilla essence
3oz plain flour
Pinch of salt

Strawberry jam

<u>Buttercream</u>
5oz butter (softened)
10oz icing sugar

In large mixing bowl, cream the butter, sugar and vanilla essence together until this is pale in colour, light, and fluffy. Sift the flour and salt, combine. Pipe stars approximately 1" wide onto a greased baking sheet, bake for about 10 minutes, these shouldn't colour up much, take care not to overbake. Cool on a wire rack. Make the buttercream by sifting the icing sugar and creaming this with the softened butter. You can add a little flavouring, e.g. vanilla essence or lemon oil. Sandwich the biscuits together with a layer of buttercream on one side and a layer of jam on the other. Dust with icing sugar or alternatively you can dip half the biscuit into melted chocolate.

Shortbread

Obviously not originating from the Black Country, but closely ingrained with baking in the region. At Christmas or New Year there was always a tin of shortbread, often bought in but sometimes homemade and homemade shortbread fresh from the oven is simply the best.

4oz Butter
2oz Caster sugar
6oz plain flour
1oz cornflour

Preheat the oven to 325°F, 170°C, 150°C Fan assisted, Gas Mark 4. Cream the butter and sugar together until light and fluffy, sift in the flour and cornflour and mix until incorporated into a ball, do not overwork or the shortbread will be hard. Flour the worktop and roll the shortbread to a large round about ¼" thick. Prick with a fork and mark the edges with a thumbprint. Transfer carefully to a greased baking sheet and bake for about 25 minutes. The shortbread should be pale gold and crisp up on cooling. Dredge with extra caster sugar and once cold store in a tin.

Scones

That ever-present staple of high tea. Contests over who baked the best scone were hotly contested as a badge of honour amongst cooks.

¾ lb self-raising flour
Pinch of salt
1 tsp bicarbonate of soda
3oz butter
3 tablespoons caster sugar
1 tablespoon lemon juice – optional
6 fl oz milk

Sift the flour into a bowl, add the salt and bicarbonate of soda. Cut in the butter and rub in until the mixture looks like fine breadcrumbs. Add the sugar and stir to mix. Warm the milk very slightly, add the lemon juice to the milk the mix this into the flour, the mix will be quite wet but if the surface is floured it should be possible to knead slightly, do not overwork and roll out about 1 ½" thick. Cut out rounds and transfer to a baking sheet. Brush with milk and bake in a preheated oven 220°C, 200°C fan assisted, Gas Mark 7 for around 10 minutes, until risen and golden. Serve, of course with strawberry jam and whipped cream, that is, if there is no clotted cream to hand.

Mint sauce

Easy to make, quick and no cooking needed, just boiling water. The sharpness of the mint cuts through the fat in lamb. Clumps of mint frequently grew by the back door, a handful picked to make the sauce on Sundays to go with the roast.

Handful of mint
Pinch of salt
Vinegar
Boiling water
Sugar

Strip the leaves from the mint stems and sprinkle with a pinch of salt. Chop finely releasing the lovely fresh smell and transfer to a small jug. Add a heaped teaspoon of sugar and around a tablespoon of boiling water to cover, enough to dissolve the sugar. Stir well. Add around two tablespoons of vinegar and taste, add more sugar, vinegar or water according to how you like your mint sauce.

Apple sauce

Most houses had at least one apple tree and apple sauce was the ideal accompaniment for home reared pork. A little cider apple vinegar can be added to give added piquancy.

4 large apples
Knob of butter
Sugar
Pinch of salt

Add a splash of water to a saucepan and place on the heat while the apples are peeled, slice roughly into the pan, add a knob of butter and a pinch of salt. Place a lid on the pan and cook until soft; this will only take a few minutes. Stir occasionally to make sure the apples don't burn to the bottom of the pan. As the apples soften, break them up into a smooth puree. Add sugar to taste, how much will depend on the type of apples, tart cookers will take much more sugar than dessert apples, stir in another knob of butter if not watching cholesterol and calories. Serve hot or cold with roast pork or on pork sandwiches.

Bread sauce

Another way of using up stale bread was bread sauce, served with roast poultry. There was rarely any bread left over in our house, but always bread sauce with chicken or turkey.

"When I was young in the early 1960's we never bought sliced bread, it was tin loaves from the bakery, wrapped in thin sheets of paper, not plastic bags. The more burnt the crust on top the better the flavour. I still look for those black tops now.

If there was any left over, it would often be grated and the crumbs stored in the freezer to make treacle tart or bread sauce. Failing that the ends of the loaf would be put in the oven as it was cooling where they would dry out, like meringues, then they were fed to the horses but only once they were crisp."

"I have fond memories of this. As a child it was my job to make it at Christmas, standing by the cooker, stirring for what felt like an age, feeding the sauce with butter, waiting for it to thicken up before transferring it to the pot shaped like a cottage loaf and adding yet more butter to the top which melted into a yellow puddle."

The sauce is equally good nearly thick enough to slice with a good onion flavour and full of butter, as it is thin and pourable. The onion can be cooked for longer in the milk, or slice it thickly before boiling to bring out more of the flavour.

"Dad always liked the onion so we used to leave it whole in the sauce, if there was any sauce left (and he hadn't eaten the onion) we would leave it in the pot until the next day when the whole lot was reheated and served up again with the leftover chicken or turkey. No one liked cloves, they tasted too much like tooth tincture."

½ pint of full cream milk
4oz white breadcrumbs (approx.) (Slightly stale bread works better than fresh)
1 onion, peeled
Salt and pepper
Cloves
Nutmeg
2oz Butter

Stud the onion with 2 or 3 cloves and place in a saucepan with the milk and nutmeg, season well. A bay leaf could also be added here for flavour and removed before the breadcrumbs are added. Simmer gently for 20 minutes or so, to flavour the milk. Add the breadcrumbs and most of the butter. Stir while heating as the sauce may stick. Let it plop and bubble while the sauce thickens. Cook for around ten minutes stirring well, as the liquid is driven off, the sauce will thicken slightly. It should taste oniony and buttery. Stir in the rest of the butter and float a little on the top to prevent a skin forming. Serve hot (or cold) with chicken.

Horseradish Sauce

Horseradish is a sturdy plant, grown in many gardens. The pungent roots, not the tough, spear-shaped leaves are grated to make horseradish sauce to accompany roast beef. So hot that when growing conditions are right, releasing the chemicals contained in the root when it is grated could sting the eyes and bring tears, but beef would not be complete without it.

Chunk of fresh horseradish root
1 tablespoon white vinegar plus soaking vinegar
Pinch of caster sugar
Pinch of mustard powder
Cream

Take a piece of horseradish root, about 2" long. Wash it well, it is worth taking the time to peel this, otherwise, there will be darker specks in the finished sauce. Grate the root on a fine side of the grater. If there is a food blender available it is worth considering using this, the root can be very strong. The more time the root is blended or once grated, the hotter it will become. Test and as soon as it is hot enough, add enough vinegar to cover the grated root completely. Leave for a few minutes then squeeze out the vinegar. If you prefer you can soak the horseradish in hot water instead of vinegar.

Mix a level tablespoon of the soaked horseradish with a tablespoon white vinegar, pinch of caster sugar, a pinch of mustard powder and dilute with enough fresh cream to give an acceptable taste and consistency.

White Sauce

"Mum would not serve cauliflower without white sauce. One day had been particularly busy, dinner was running late and there was a rush to get it to the table. The plates were already on their way to the dining room as she realised the cauliflower was naked. Panic followed, plates were bustled back to the kitchen and kept hot while a pan of sauce was whisked up in record time and peace was restored."

This is a standard roux, flour is cooked with butter, milk added to thin, then seasoned. Great poured over cauliflower or as the basis for cheese, onion or mushroom sauce.

1oz flour
1oz butter
1 pint milk
Seasoning

Melt the butter in a pan, a frying pan will give more room to whisk. Add the flour and cook for a few minutes. Not long, one or two minutes should be long enough. Take the pan off the heat and slacken the sauce with a little milk, whisk in the rest of the milk. Put the pan back on the heat and slowly bring to the boil, turn down to a simmer until the sauce thickens, season.

Cheese Sauce

Use the above recipe, once the sauce has thickened take it off the heat and stir in 4oz cheese, stir to melt the cheese but do not reheat. Perfect for cauliflower cheese, pour it over boiled cauliflower in a heatproof dish and sprinkle a little grated cheese over the top. Decorate with sliced tomato and transfer to a medium oven until the cauliflower is hot and the sauce browned.

Onion Sauce

1oz flour
1oz butter
1 pint of milk
1 bay leaf
¼ teaspoon of peppercorns
1 onion

Put the milk into a pan add the bay leaf, peppercorns and heat gently for 10 minutes. Remove the bay leaf and the peppercorns. Peel and finely chop the onion. Heat the butter in a frying pan, fry the onion over a gentle heat until very soft, add seasoning and the flour, a little more butter can be added if necessary. Stir in the flour and cook for a minute or two, Take off the heat and blend in the milk a little at a time, return to the heat, bring to the boil, then turn the heat down and simmer until the sauce thickens. If a smoother sauce is preferred, it can be blended then reheated.

Parsley Sauce

Tinned salmon was not only served in sandwiches, it was also popular with sweet, green peas and new potatoes cloaked in parsley sauce. Parsley sauce also works well with salty gammon steaks. Biennial curly leaved parsley with its distinctive taste and high vitamin C content was present in many gardens waiting to make its way to the dinner table.

Simple parsley sauce
1oz butter
1oz flour
1 pint milk
3 tablespoons chopped parsley
Salt
Pepper

Melt the butter over a gentle heat and stir in the flour, cook for a couple of minutes then gradually add the milk whisking as you go. If the sauce starts to become lumpy, take it off the heat and a knob of butter and whisk with a balloon whisk. Bring to the boil, and then turn down the heat. Cook until thickened, season and add the parsley.

Cucumber and onion in vinegar (Vinegar salad)

"Always reminds me going to my grans for Sunday tea but she would put sliced tomatoes in hers as well......."

"Gran always put Tomatoes in as well. Lovely. We had tinned peaches with Carnation milk, and bread an' butter to mop up the juice....delicious...oh dear dribbling."

"We always had this for Sunday tea. I can still remember the taste of it. With salmon sandwiches. Followed by tinned fruit and condensed milk. Always served up in a heavy glass bowl. "

Spanish (large) onion
Cucumber
Pinch sugar
Vinegar

Slice the cucumber and the onion into very thin slices, as thin as possible. Layer in a dish and top up with enough vinegar to cover. Sometimes a pinch of sugar is added to the vinegar to enhance the flavour.

"We often had this with tea, always made in the same flat Pyrex dish, only about half an inch deep, white with ducks decorating the bottom and good old-fashioned malt vinegar."

Stuffing

There are many types of stuffing including parsley and thyme or chestnut, but by far, the most versatile is sage and onion. Forcemeat stuffing is a mixture of minced meat, generally sausage meat and vegetables, usually onions. A chicken is not complete without it! Stuffing the bird is not a new idea, it pre-dates the Black Country and can be traced back to Roman times, must be good to have been practised for so many years. Simple to prepare, homemade stuffing outshines shop-bought every time.

2 large onions
4 sausages
4 tablespoons breadcrumbs
Few fresh sage leaves
Seasoning

Many recipes call for an egg yolk to help the mix. Boil the onions until soft; add the sage leaves for a minute or so, just to take the edge off the flavour, which can be strong. Chop the onions very finely with the sage; you can use a food processor for this. Skin the sausages and add to the onions with the breadcrumbs. Season. Add a knob of butter and enough boiling water to mix to a soft (not wet) consistency. Use this to stuff the cavities on poultry or shape into balls and cook in a roasting pan with the potatoes around a joint. Or it can be cooked in an ovenproof dish for around half an hour until the top is crisp and browned, then served along with whichever meat is on the menu. Traditionally served with poultry and pork.

Mustards

Years ago, the available range of mustards was nothing like there is today. The hot yellow condiment, which was always Colman's mustard came as a dry powder and was freshly mixed using a spot of milk for every meal. The hot qualities of mustard were believed to not only improve digestion but also improve the circulation and hot mustard baths where the mustard powder was added to the water were believed to help alleviate aches, pains, and rheumatism or restore those suffering from the cold. Mustard oil, produced when the seeds are ground for the condiment was in great demand as a skin rub for rheumatism, similar to liniment in its effect.

Preserving a way of life

Preserving was a way of life in the days before freezers, different coloured contents of the jars marked the passing of the year. Marmalade from bitter Seville oranges in the dark winter months, the vibrant orange of the preserve a reminder of the sun to come. The short days after Christmas were a time to consume the fruits of earlier labours stored in the larder, until the days lengthened and the harvests began again. Berries and stone fruits for jams, apples for chutneys, onions for pickling, beans for brining, all filling up the shelves once again.

Pickled onions

A well-kept secret by those who pickle, from those who don't, is just how simple it is to stock the larder with your very own onions steeped in vinegar. So simple, even for me, that a well-established autumn ritual involves jars, brewed condiment and alliums. You will also be pleased to know that onions are one of the world's healthiest foods. As soon as the strawberries are over (which is much too early), eyes are peeled for red string nets bulging with tiny onions which start to appear around September.

Cocktail onions are small onions, the very small ones, about ½" in diameter these are easy to eat, but take forever to prepare, an awful lot are needed to fill a jar and even more to fill several jars, but the result is worth it. Far speedier to do are good, old-fashioned pickling onions, about 1" across and much quicker to fill a basin as you peel them.

All manner of ingredients can be added to liven up a good old-fashioned jar of pickled onions; chillies, honey, sugar, pickling spice the choice is virtually limitless, but they are first rate as they come, plain and simple, just onion and vinegar.

An ideal accompaniment to lots of things! Salads, sandwiches even fish and chips.

There are two methods of pickling, dry and wet; one involves layering the onions in salt, the other soaking in brine. Dry pickling is rumoured to give a crisper result.

The only drawback to home pickled onions is the smell that will haunt you for days, the aroma of onions impregnated into the skin on the hands; thankfully, this is not altogether unpleasant.

1 tbsp salt to 1 pint water
Pickling onions – as many as you can stand to do, they'll probably eat more
Pickling spice or flavouring of your choice

Fill a four-pint basin with cold water and add 4 tablespoons of salt. Top and tail the onions and peel off the papery brown outer later. Put the onions into the brine and leave them for between 24 hours and three days, cover the bowl with a plate to prevent any flies from taking a bath in the brine.

If the weather is warmer, take the onions out of the brine after around 24 hours rather than leave them for longer.
Take them out of the water and dry then transfer to a sterilised wide neck jar, when the jar is full, pour in good quality vinegar making sure all the onions are submerged. Screw the top on tight and wait. Try to give them a couple of weeks to mature, but they are, apparently fine to eat within a matter of hours!

Some people heat the vinegar with pickling spices, a few chilli flakes or other flavourings then pour this over hot.

Pickled Red Cabbage

Red cabbage is a much-neglected vegetable. It is so simple to pickle that anyone can do it and the ruby coloured cabbage looks so pretty in the jar, but don't just leave it at pickled cabbage, it deserves far more. A far cry from floppy over boiled green cabbage served up with Sunday lunch, red cabbage braised with apple and onion, livened up with brown sugar and vinegar adds new depth to winter food. Choose a fresh cabbage, the heavier the better in relation to its size and look for crisp leaves that haven't begun to wilt. Pickled red cabbage is not a particularly long-lived pickle but if prepared in small batches, you probably won't need to worry about waste.

Red cabbage
Salt
Vinegar

You can use ready-spiced pickling vinegar or add your own spices and a little sugar, but plain vinegar allows the cabbage to be the star.

Remove the outer leaves of the cabbage and feed them to the rabbit if you have one, next doors if you don't. Slice the cabbage into quarters, then into thin shreds, discarding the hard white core. Layer this in a large bowl with a good sprinkling of salt between each layer, a tablespoon of salt or so should be enough on each layer. Cover and leave overnight, by morning the cabbage will have turned a delightful shade of blue. Rinse the salt off the cabbage and dry before packing into clean jars. Fill the jars with vinegar making sure all the cabbage is submerged. Put the lid on and store in a cool place for a few days before eating.

Pickled Eggs

Just like vegetables, chickens are seasonal creatures. A good layer will produce an egg nearly every day throughout the summer, but as the days shorten, the eggs will become fewer. It follows there will be more eggs than can be used sometimes, and in true Black Country fashion, waste not want not, along with onions and cabbage, eggs can be pickled. No fish and chip shop counter would have been complete without a large jar of pickled eggs.

Eggs
Vinegar

Hard boil as many eggs as you want to pickle, 10 - 15 minutes in boiling water should be long enough. Drain and cool quickly by running them under cold water to prevent a dark ring forming around the yolk. Peel the eggs and put them in a large, clean jar. Cover with vinegar. Distilled (white) vinegar will give a similar result to "chip shop" pickled eggs but traditional brown malt vinegar works just as well and is a cheaper option.

Pickled Damsons

Another family stalwart, pickled damson are not very common these days and not often available commercially but the sharp flavour partners cold meats or a ploughman's salad beautifully.

2lbs damsons
½ pint white vinegar
2lb sugar
Cinnamon stick
3 or 4 cloves (optional)

You can reduce the amount of sugar slightly if the pickle is preferred more tart. This also works well using malt vinegar and brown sugar. Wipe the damsons over with a piece of kitchen roll, don't wash if they don't need it, and remove the stalks. The fruit is best picked on a dry day from somewhere well away from roads. Heat the vinegar with the sugar and spices until the sugar has dissolved; leave to cool with the spices in for a stronger flavour. Remove the spices from the vinegar and discard. Prick the damsons all over with a darning needle or a fork taking care not to split the skins, add them to the vinegar in the pan and heat gently until the fruit softens slightly, try not to stir too much or the fruit will break up, try to keep it as whole as possible. Remove from heat and place into jars. Pour the cooking liquid over as it is, or boil this for a little longer to reduce, before adding it to the fruit.

Piccalilli

This has a characteristic yellow colour from mustard in the sauce, those who don't like the distinctive taste of English mustard will not appreciate the taste of piccalilli. Some people swear by a particular mix of vegetables, but use what's available, that was the whole point of preserving, to preserve the excess harvest. Choose for personal preference to make up the weight. This could contain cucumbers, cauliflower, carrot, dwarf beans, tomato, peppers; small silverskin onions are rather good, the list is almost endless. The resulting product should be crisp and tasty, more of a pickle than a chutney; the vegetables are salted rather than cooked thus retaining the fresh quality.

2kg vegetables, choose from cauliflower, courgette, cucumber, dwarf green beans, green or yellow tomatoes, carrots, silverskin onions, peppers.
2 tablespoons of salt
2 tablespoons of coriander seed
2 tablespoons cumin seed
1 tablespoon turmeric
2 tablespoons mustard seed
3 tablespoons mustard powder
5 tablespoons cornflour
1 ½ pints cider vinegar
8oz sugar
4oz honey

Wash and peel the vegetables as appropriate then cut them into small, bite-sized chunks. Sprinkle with the salt and mix well, so all are evenly coated. Cover and leave somewhere cool overnight. By morning, brine will have formed, drain this and rinse the vegetables well in cold water.

Mix the cornflour, coriander, cumin, turmeric, mustard seed and mustard powder with enough vinegar to make a smooth paste. Put the rest of the vinegar in a large pan over low heat with the sugar and the honey until the sugar has dissolved, add the paste and simmer for a few minutes until thickened and fragrant. Take off the heat, stir in the vegetables and put into jars while hot. Store for four weeks before consuming. Who am I kidding? Doesn't taste too bad as soon as it's cooled!

Apple Chutney

Simple, easy chutney recipe that uses up windfalls or eats into the autumn glut of apples.

1 tablespoon olive oil
1 ¼ lb/500g onions - peeled and chopped
1 ¼ lb/500g apples - peeled, cored and chopped
10 fl oz/300ml red wine vinegar
4oz/100g granulated sugar
8oz/200g dark brown soft sugar
1 teaspoon ground cinnamon
1/2 teaspoon ground nutmeg
1/4 teaspoon ground allspice
1/4 teaspoon cayenne pepper or chilli powder
1 pinch salt

In a large saucepan, gently heat the olive oil, add the onion, cook over a low heat until soft, translucent, and starting to caramelise, stirring occasionally, do not let it brown too much. Add the remaining ingredients. Bring to the boil, reduce heat, and cover. Simmer 30 minutes, stirring frequently, until the apples are tender.

Take off the heat and immediately spoon the chutney into hot, sterilised jars and seal. Once cold, store in a cool, dark place. After opening, chutney should easily keep 3 to 4 weeks in the fridge.

Salted Green Beans

Runner beans are a great addition to the vegetable garden, cropping heavily over a number of weeks. Freshly picked beans go from plant to pan in a matter of minutes, boil quickly and produce tender green slithers to grace any meal. Because they crop so well and are so easy to grow on their tall canes there will often be more produce than a family can eat. To preserve the glut is much easier since the advent of freezers. Pick, slice, blanch, freeze, done. In the times before freezers, one way of preserving beans was salting. There were two methods, using a brine or layering with salt. The high salt content should kill most bacteria, though there have been very infrequent issues with salting beans; these are generally related to methods of preserving where the beans are fermented, not the method given here.

<u>Salt pot beans</u>
Easy and quick to prepare, make sure you only use the youngest, most tender beans and the results will beat frozen, hands down. If there not enough to fill the pot initially, add to the pot as the beans are harvested over time.

Green beans
Salt

Use a wide-mouthed pot so the beans can easily be removed for use, and preferably a pot rather than a jar as this needs to be kept away from light. Alternatively, wrap the jar in brown paper. Check over the beans, discarding any blemished ones. Place a layer of salt in the bottom of the pot. String the beans and lay them on the salt. Pack these down well and add another layer of salt. Fill the pot with layers of salt and beans; this can be done over a number of days. A brine will form which will preserve the beans through to the winter. Store in a cool place and check occasionally to make sure they are still covered by the brine. Remove any film that may form on the top.

To use remove from the brine and rinse well. Soak in cold water to remove the excess salt but for no longer than two hours or they will become tough. Use as normal.

Bottom oven beetroot

Beetroot, freshly pulled from the dark earth has a wonderfully sweet quality. Cooked to perfection it is soft and yielding as the fork goes in, but not so soft as to put up no fight at all. There was always room for beetroot in the vegetable garden; it matures quickly, cropping at six weeks in a good year. Very much underrated, not helped by the fact that often the only experience people have of beetroot, is when it has been drowned in coarse vinegar and all the colour and taste leached out leaving a dull brown shadow of its former self.

Beetroot washed and put into the bottom oven of a Rayburn within minutes of being cooked, retains much of the sweetness and can be left overnight, taken out the following morning and served as a vegetable in its own right or peeled and placed into jars. The larger beets need slicing, smaller ones about an inch across are fine as they are. The jars can then be topped up with malt vinegar, which will turn a delightful shade of purple and stored until needed to supplement the winter diet.

Fruit was often in abundance at certain times of the year, there would be fruit trees in gardens or on allotments, even wild food could be collected. Gooseberry bushes, red or green would produce lots of hairy berries that taste better cooked than raw, but when there were more than could be eaten, the excess would be preserved, one method was to make jam. Gooseberry jam is not commonly available on a commercial basis but these fat berries make better jam than is usually expected, worth trying if there is access to a few pounds.

Blackcurrant bushes were another common addition; these also cropped heavily providing an overabundance of fruit. Damson trees would mark boundaries or punctuate hedges, brambles would line the lanes. Strawberries have a short cropping season and don't last long once picked, but they do make exceedingly good jam.

Strawberry Jam

Jewel red, summer in a jar. The taste of homemade jam is on a par with any premium brand and there is the smug satisfaction in every bite of knowing it's homemade. Strawberry jam has a reputation for being tricky to set, but it's worth the effort and the worst that can happen is to end up with a vat of rich, syrupy strawberry sauce, still perfect for trifles.

2lbs strawberries
2lbs sugar, white granulated is fine
Juice of a lemon
Knob of butter

Pick over the strawberries and discard any that are overripe or soft. Don't wash them but wipe over with kitchen roll if you need to, if you wash them they may turn mushy and the jam will be more difficult to set. Hull the fruit and place in a large bowl, add the sugar and the lemon juice. Leave overnight. Tip into a preserving pan or a large heavy-based saucepan and heat gently until all the sugar has dissolved, make sure there are no sugar crystals left, even on the side. If these get into the cooked jam, the sugar in the jam may crystallise out.

Increase the temperature and boil rapidly, if any scum forms on the top skim it off the surface of the jam as it appears. Setting point for jams is 105°C, once the jam reaches temperature, pull it off the heat, stir in the butter and allow it to cool slightly before filling sterilised jars. To test for a set without a thermometer use the wrinkle test. Put a plate in the freezer before you start or pop a couple of ice cubes on a plate to chill it. After about ten minutes boiling, begin to test for a set at regular intervals by dropping a little jam onto the plate. Push it with your finger and if the surface wrinkles, the jam is done. Take the jam off the heat while you test it. As it nears setting point you will often notice a change in the consistency of the jam as it darkens and thickens, the bubbles will change too. If the jam is boiled for too long, it might go past the setting point.

Cool for a few minutes in the pan, removing any remaining scum, once cool enough to handle transfer to sterilised jars, put the lid on while still hot and label the jars.

Damson Jam

Something of an underdog but nonetheless a king among jams. There is a special sharpness, less sweet than strawberry jam and packed full of flavour, damson jam often does not receive the recognition it deserves. The fruit is much higher in pectin than strawberries so this should be more reliable to set and often gives a firmer set. Many Black Country gardens had one or more damson trees standing alone or forming part of a boundary hedge. They take up relatively little room but crop heavily most years. The sight of the purple fruit in September is always welcome.

3lbs damsons
3lbs sugar

Pick over the damsons and discard any soft or split fruits, remove the stalks. Place in a pan with a spot of water, barely enough to cover the bottom of the pan. Heat gently; stirring occasionally to make sure the fruit does not catch until it starts to release the juices. Press the fruit against the sides of the pan as it begins to soften to release the stones. Simmer until the skins are soft. Add the sugar and simmer until the sugar has completely dissolved. The stones will rise to the surface as the jam cooks, showing up as pale almond shapes in a purple lake. Remove as many of these tooth breakers are you can and any scum that surfaces. Once the sugar has dissolved turn up the heat, boil rapidly until the set point is reached (see Strawberry jam recipe for details of this), and transfer to jars when this has cooled slightly. The jam can be passed through a plastic sieve to remove the skins and any remaining stones if you don't mind losing a little of the jam.

Marmalade

Marmalade can be made at any time of year, but in January, knobbly, thick skinned, bitter Seville oranges appear in the shops, mouth puckeringly sour, they don't make for pleasant eating, but they do make amazing marmalade. Sharp and strong flavoured, the resulting amber conserve is wonderful spread on toast, in cakes, on a steamed pudding or even as at topping for a roast ham. The flavour depends slightly on the temperature of the set, around 219°F, 104°C, the set will be soft, even runny but the flavour fresh and orangey. 220°F, 105°C, gives a better set, still fresh, the bitterness coming through. By 222°F, 106°C, the flavour will have more pronounced caramel notes, the colour darker, a firm set and the peel will start to become tough.

3lbs Seville oranges
2 lemons
6lb sugar

5 pints water

Wash the oranges, and put these into a large pan with the lemon juice and the water. Bring to a simmer and put a lid on, simmer until the skin is tender, don't rush this part, the skins need to cook to release the pectin and to be tender enough to eat. Once the sugar goes in later, they won't release much more pectin. They could go into the oven at around 140°C for this stage, or into the Aga. Take the oranges out of the water when the skins are tender and cool in a bowl, do not discard the water in which they were boiled.

When they are cool enough to handle, cut the oranges in half, remove the insides and add to the pan along with any juice or other liquid. Pull as much of the pith away from the peel as you can and throw it in the pan. Put the pan back onto the heat and boil rapidly, aim to reduce the amount of liquid by around a third. Strain the liquid through a nylon sieve, pressing the contents well to remove as much of the pectin as you can, then throw away the pulp.

Slice the orange peel into shreds; add these to the preserving pan along with the water and the sugar. Simmer, stirring, until the sugar has completely dissolved, there should be no trace of sugar grains in the marmalade or they will act as seeds for the dissolved sugar to crystallise out on, and crunchy marmalade is not nice on toast.

Turn up the heat and boil the marmalade until it reaches setting point. Try not to stir it too much while boiling. When it's close to the setting point, there may be a change in the bubbles from a rich froth, to larger, steadier bubbles. On a jam thermometer, the setting point should be at 105°C, 220°F. If you do not have a jam thermometer try the wrinkle test. Place a plate in the freezer before you start, when you think the jam is near to setting point take the plate out of the freezer and drop a little jam on the plate, wait for it to cool and push it with your finger, if the surface wrinkles the marmalade is ready. There is also the flake test. Stir the marmalade with a wooden spoon, so the spoon is completely coated, then hold this vertically over the pan, if the marmalade is ready, the liquid will run down the spoon and form a drop on the end, it will not drip back into the pan unless you shake the spoon. Take the pan off the heat when testing for set point, in case the marmalade cooks too far.

When setting point is reached, take the pan off the heat and leave to settle for about 15 minutes, then transfer to clean, sterilised jars, be careful the marmalade will still be hot. Fill pots right to the top and put the lid on while still hot, this way there will be a vacuum created in the jar.

Marmalade should keep well, for years in fact. Seville oranges also freeze well whole, so can be kept to prepare the marmalade at a later date.

Lemon Curd

Dating back at least to Victorian times, this is much easier to make than possibly people would expect, sharp and thick, a great filling for individual tarts also good for using up eggs, quicker to prepare than jams or marmalades too.

4 unwaxed lemons
8oz caster sugar
3oz butter
2 eggs plus two egg yolks

Wash the lemons. Peel the zest from the lemons and muddle this with the sugar to impart some of the flavour into the sugar. Remove the zest. Some recipes include a little lemon zest. If there is no problem losing the smooth texture of the curd, chop a little of the zest very finely, or grate this from the lemon using one of the smaller sides of the grater.

Juice the lemons. Beat the butter and sugar until very light and fluffy; you could use an electric whisk for this. Gradually whisk in the eggs and egg yolks, then add the lemon juice. The mixture will curdle but keep going.

Heat gently in a bowl over a pan of water or in a heavy based pan to spread the heat evenly, don't let this boil or the result might be scrambled egg. As the mixture begins to look smooth, increase the heat but still don't allow this to boil, cook until it thickens. If you have a jam thermometer test the temperature, it should only rise to about 170°F, 77°C. When the mixture has thickened enough to coat the back of the wooden spoon and leave a trail in the pan, take it off the heat and stir in the lemon zest if this is being included. Cool, a skin will form on the top of the curd as would happen with custard; cover the surface with Clingfilm to prevent this. The curd will thicken further as it cools. Store in the fridge, this does not have the keeping properties of jam but will last for about a week if stored covered in the fridge.

Mincemeat

The first batch of mince pies signifies the start of Christmas, hot and fragrant out of the oven, covered with a light dusting of icing sugar. Homemade mincemeat is easy to make and great for little ones to help to stir. Don't be afraid to double the quantities here, you will probably still run out way before Christmas. The smell as this is stirred and the fragrance that lingers evoke memories of Christmas past to be enjoyed in Christmas present; spice, fruit and alcohol. There is absolutely nothing wrong with a good quality shop bought mincemeat, especially livened up with extra rum or brandy, or orange juice for those whose don't, but there is a certain satisfaction biting into a mince pie made from homemade pastry and your own mincemeat. Childhood memories abound of mothers in a "pinna," flour-covered arms wielding a rolling pin with love.

1lb currants
1lb raisins

1lb sultanas
1 large cooking apple, (Bramley works well)
2oz almonds
12oz demerara sugar
4oz soft dark brown sugar
2 x 8oz boxes suet
1 level tsp cinnamon
3 heaped tsp mixed spice
Grating of nutmeg
8oz candied peel
1 orange
1 lemon
8 tablespoons brandy
4 tablespoons rum

Wash the dried fruit by placing into a colander and rinsing under the cold tap, dry in a tea towel. The dried fruit on sale today probably does not need rinsing so this stage could probably be omitted, but as creatures of habit, fruit is often still rinsed in the Black Country. Peel and core the apple, chop into small pieces, likewise the almonds, chop these finely too. Orange, lemon or both can be used, the zest is needed and the juice, use a fine setting on the grater to grate the zest from the fruit or peel thinly, leaving the pith behind, slice into slithers or chop finely. Chop the candid peel finely.

Soak the dried fruits in the brandy to plump up. Remove from the brandy and put all the fruit and the nuts into a large bowl, add the spices, sugar and suet, mix well, then pour in the spirits with the lemon/orange juice and mix again. This can be left for 24 hours before packing into jars, stir now and then throughout the day. Pack down into sterilised jars; push down to make sure there are no air pockets. Put the lid on and store for two weeks to mellow before using. The blend of fruit is not critical, if peel is not liked, leave it out, if currants are preferred use more of these, the alcohol can be increased too. Vegetarian suet also works; butter can be substituted for suet.

The flavour is best within 6 months or so but should keep until the next Christmas if stored in a cool, dark place.

Sometimes, you may find the apple is too juicy which makes the mincemeat too wet and opening the possibility it may ferment during storage. One method is to put the fruit mix into a low oven for three hours, then allow to cool completely before adding the spirits and bottling, the suet or butter will melt down covering the fruit, which will stop the fresh fruit weeping in storage.

Odds… and well you've guessed it - things I couldn't find a home for anywhere else

There were all manner of foods and snacks consumed in the Black Country, as we've already seen, every part of the pig, inside and out; ears, snouts, tails, feet, intestines, nothing was safe from the pot. Food was eaten fresh or dried, pickled or salted to preserve it. There were jams and chutneys to grace the table. But pre-1960 what do you feed a hungry child between meals. Not biscuits or sweets, McDonald's would not cross the pond for years yet the same was true of Kentucky. Garden produce was good to chew on!

<u>Rhubarb and sugar.</u>
Sticks of rhubarb pulled fresh from the plant, leaves removed and the cut end of the stalk dipped into granulated white sugar.

<u>Butter and sugar</u>
A less healthy option was a mix of butter and sugar, eaten as was. This is also good on Yorkshire pudding – without the gravy.

<u>Sugar sandwiches</u>
Buttered bread with a sprinkling of white sugar as a filling

<u>Sauce sandwiches</u>
Brown sauce or tomato ketchup spread thinly over the bread, nothing else bar sauce and bread.

Anything slapped between two pieces of bread was fair game, syrup sandwiches, cake sandwiches even sausage roll sandwiches.

<u>Sterilising jars</u>
This would not represent a sterile jar in surgical terms but should do well enough for jam. Wash the jars and lids in hot, soapy water making sure they are clean and free from any damage (cracks or

chips), rinse well to remove all traces of soap. Place into a preheated oven, 140ºC– 180ºC, while still wet for 15 minutes. Fill while both the jam or chutney and the jars are still hot.

Alternatively, run the clean jars and lids through the dishwasher on a hot cycle (no detergent), or you can boil the jars and lids for 20 minutes or half fill them with water and microwave for long enough to boil the water for 1 minute

Piece

It was always a piece of dripping or a piece of bread and jam, never a slice or a piece of bread – just a piece.

Many types of home-grown produce could be and would be turned into alcohol. Households made their own wine and beer. A back garden brew 'us would be pressed into service to make beer for the family or several families. Hops bines ran up tin wires in the garden. Green, cone-shaped flowers flavoured the beer, giving the bitter taste; they also improved the keeping qualities of the beer.

"Hop flowers felt like paper when they were dried. Nan would make hop pillows, stuffing a few dried hop flowers into a pillowcase, she said it was to help you sleep, but the rustle of the dried flowers would keep me awake."

All manner of things were saved to make wine, pea pods collected by the neighbours were handed on furtively at the gatepost after dark for a batch of pea pod wine. It takes a lot of pods for a gallon of wine and patience is needed. Don't rush this one, it's more than capable of stripping the enamel from teeth if consumed too young. Another lass was caught unawares by the strength of homemade parsnip wine, which is by no means unique in its ability to induce inebriation from the feet up, but it is very good at it. Everything is fine until the drinker tries to stand.

Elderberries and damsons gave rise to some powerful reds. Wheat and raisins give a result similar to sweet sherry, smooth and luscious, and orange wine is also well worth making for something different.

Damson gin

Another way of using up the glut of damsons in a good year.

"Every year in September I make a batch of damson gin. It keeps for a year or so I'm told. I disagree; I find it doesn't keep well at all. When I check on it just before Christmas to adjust the sugar, before I take the gin off the fruit, more often than not it has evaporated and only the fruit is left in the jar. So I'd go as far as to say it doesn't keep at all! After making it for years, I've never caught the culprit."

Following on from the above comment, if tamper proof lids are available, it pays to make more damson gin than you think you will need in the first year. That way the results can be sipped and savoured, compared, year by year. The flavour of the gin improves with keeping. In our house, this has never been possible. If it does happen that the gin has escaped by Christmas, or once it has been syphoned off the fruits, this can be replaced with sherry for a "double crop."

1lb damsons
Around 6oz sugar, ordinary white granulated is fine
Gin

Use a clean, ideally sterile jar, if possible large enough to hold a bottle of gin, but there's no hard and fast rule to ingredients or proportions, just damsons, gin and sugar so the size of the container really doesn't matter too much. The neck should be wide enough to add the fruit and sugar easily.

Check through the damsons one by one and remove any stalks. Wipe over and prick several times with a darning needle or cocktail stick, place the fruit in the jar. Add the sugar and put the top on the jar. Give the jar a shake a couple of times a day and that's it. Try to keep in a cool dark place or cover the jar if it is made with clear glass, this will help preserve the vibrant, rich purple colour given by the skins.

Taste every so often and tweak the amount of sugar, some people prefer this dry, others sweet and syrupy. By Christmas, it should be well on the way to drink.

When you are happy with the flavour, strain the gin off the fruit into a clean bottle. Try to store a while before consuming if possible, as the flavour will improve.

The gin is ok left on the fruit for several months, but best not left much longer than six months before straining. This makes lovely a warming liqueur, great for sipping at Christmas or filling hip flasks.

Elderflower Champagne

Champagne might be a little of an overstatement and a term not allowed under EU rules, but this is the Black Country and this is Elderflower Champagne. The beautiful froth of cream flower heads appearing on Elder trees from the middle of May, can be turned into an effervescent, elderflower-scented taste of summer in a bottle. It is alcoholic but only just. The elderflowers make their own fizz from natural yeast present on the flowers. An elderly gentleman let slip the recipe, it was, I believe, his sister's and though they are both long gone now their elderflower champagne lives on.

5 heads elderflowers
1 lemon
4 pints cold water, ideally bottled
9oz sugar
1tbsp white wine or cider vinegar

Pick the heads of elder on the morning of a warm sunny day; the flowers should be dry. Collect from areas well away from roads or factories, which will ensure the blossoms aren't affected by pollution.

Don't wash them just shake off any bugs. The flowers must be very fresh. Young heads where the flowers have not long opened, otherwise, instead of the lovely floral scent, the character will be different and altogether less pleasant. Use them as soon as you can after picking.

In a large, scrupulously clean container, dissolve the sugar in the water, this may need warming for the sugar to fully dissolve, slice the lemon and put this in too. Cool completely before adding the elderflowers and the vinegar. Stir gently; cover the container and leave to stand for one day, stirring several times throughout the day and every day until the flowers are removed. Check to see if this is fermenting, there should be bubbles and the beginnings of froth on the top hopefully after one day, or if the weather is cooler by the end of the second day or third day. Natural yeasts present on the surface of the flowers cause the fermentation process, put an ear over the container and listen, you should be able to hear this.

After three days, remove the flowers. If there are no signs of fermentation by then, you could add a pinch of yeast. Leave the champagne for another couple of days, then strain and bottle into sterilised, screw top bottles. If necessary, this could be left longer before bottling. Check the taste and adjust the sugar if necessary. The yeast will still be working and as a by-product of fermentation it will produce carbon dioxide, so do not overtighten the tops on the bottles or they may explode.

The champagne will be ready to drink in less than a week from start to finish. It won't keep for long and will become drier as the yeast ferments out the sugar. Serve chilled.

If possible used bottled rather than tap water, as this will be chemical free, if it has to be tap water allow it to stand overnight if possible, to reduce the chlorine levels.

Parsnip wine

A surplus of produce had to be used somehow and what else would you do with a glut of parsnips? It may not sound that appetising compared to today's fine, foreign wines but there are some good Parsnip wines. Parsnips are best left in the ground until after the first frost so they say, to sweeten them up and as vegetables go parsnips are already sweet. This, together with the sugar added in the recipe can make a strong wine. Reputedly, strong enough to go straight to the legs. Once upon a time, granny had to be supported on the journey home, propped up on each side in her thoroughly cheerful state, after just a couple of glasses of parsnip wine. Sadly, she is no longer with us to give further details of this particular batch of home-made wine.

4lbs parsnips
3lbs sugar
One gallon water
2 lemons
2 oranges
Sachet of wine yeast, try sauternes yeast
Handful of chopped raisins

Wash the parsnips but do not peel. Chop these into chunks and put into a large pan with the orange and lemon peel (no pith). Fill the pan with water and boil until the parsnips are just cooked. Do not overcook these. Strain the liquid into a wine bucket, the parsnips are not needed again for the wine, but you can boil them further, roast them, make soup with them, mash them, but do not waste them – it does not fit with Black Country food ethos.

Add the sugar, enough water to make up to a gallon and the chopped raisins. Start the yeast according to the instructions on the packet and add to the bucket when the water is cool enough, around blood heat, too hot and it will kill the yeast. Leave in the bucket for four or five days, stirring every day. Fermentation should be obvious by the end of the five days, there should be froth on top and little bubbles will be working their way to the surface. Strain into a demi-john and top up with cooled, boiled water. Add an airlock to the top and be patient until it stops bubbling. Syphon the wine off the sediment into a clean demijohn and check for signs of fermentation. Wait until the wine clears, bottle into clean, sterilised bottles and leave for a year before drinking.

Ginger beer

"The night was pleasantly warm, but not so hot as to make sleep difficult, the house was dark and quiet. Only the deep breathing of a golden retriever asleep in the kitchen broke the silence. Bang, the dog was awake. Bang, bang, BANG. Lights flashed on, everyone was awake. Hushed voices replaced the quiet. "Is it someone breaking in?" whispered mum, eyes wide. "Sounded more like gunshots," muttered dad. BANG. "It's coming from downstairs!" Gingerly, one stair at a time, everyone crept down to the hall. "There's a noise in the kitchen." There was a flood in the pantry too. Ginger beer all over the floor, the warm weather had woken up the yeast and the bottles exploded. This was the first of many episodes to come. Mum used to make ginger beer regularly and regularly we would be roused at night by the sound of bottles exploding when she forgot to release the pressure. The ginger beer plant in its little jam jar used to sit on the pantry windowsill waiting to be fed with a spoonful of sugar and ginger. The taste, though, was hit and miss."

To make your own authentic ginger beer, firstly you will need a ginger beer plant. Fifty years ago these were everywhere, tops of fridges, pantry shelves, over the boiler in the kitchen. So common, they could not be given away. The ginger beer plant would be halved every time a batch was made resulting in a glut a GBPs (that's ginger beer plants).

There are "proper ginger beer plants" which are made up of a culture of a particular type of yeast found naturally growing on ginger, together with a certain strain of lactobacillus bacteria. It is potluck trying to breed this mix at home but they are available commercially if they can be sourced, generally from the internet. Instructions are given for those foolhardy, sorry, brave enough to try. Alternatively, a brewer's yeast can be used and both methods are given below.

The ginger beer plant has a long pedigree, as far back as the 1700's Henry Marshall identified the organisms that co-exist so people today can produce lashings of ginger beer.

The authentic Ginger Beer Plant (SCOBY – Symbiotic culture of bacteria and yeast) is based on *Saccharomyces florentinus.* This is the yeast potential ginger beer plant producers are hoping to culture, along with *Lactobacillus hilgardii* but it's down to luck whether these are the ones that will be present on the ginger and as they are microscopic, it's difficult to ask them their parentage. How to decide what is actually growing in the culture without access to a fair range of microbiological testing equipment is problematic. Added to which names of bacteria and yeast seem to change with alarming frequency.

The bacteria produce a sort of jelly-like gloop in which the yeast cells live and the yeast produces alcohol, which the bacteria seem to rather like, so if the pairing is right, this is a win-win partnership that works for both of them.

<u>Authentic ginger beer plant (or not depending on what grows!)</u>

1 tablespoon of fresh root ginger, chopped
2 teaspoons granulated sugar
Bottled water

Put the finely chopped ginger into a sterilised wide mouthed jar. Add the sugar and cover this to prevent flies and bugs making their home in there too. A piece of muslin or part of a pair of tights secured over the neck of the jar with an elastic band is ideal, as this will let the air in but keep the beasties out. Leave somewhere where it will be at room temperature, not too hot, not too cold, a shaded windowsill or kitchen shelf. Feed every day with two teaspoons of sugar and two teaspoons of chopped ginger. Take a look at this after a week, it should smell pleasant and there should be signs of the yeast working, froth on the top. If it smells unpleasant or there is any trace of mould, throw it away and try again.

<u>Fake Fermented (Brewer's yeast) Ginger Beer Plant</u>
½ tsp dried yeast
1 tsp ground ginger
1 tsp sugar
Warm water

Mix all the dry ingredients in a jar and half fill with warm water, about blood heat, not too hot or the yeast will be killed. Cover as in the above recipe and feed in the same way with a teaspoon of sugar and a teaspoon of ginger every day for a week. The water needs to be chlorine free, either bottled water can be used or add the juice of a lemon to remove the chlorine from tap water.

Ginger beer

1 tablespoon of your ginger beer plant
1 lemon - juice only
10oz sugar
2 tsp ground ginger
¼ tsp cream of tartar – this regulates the acidity but could be left out
3 ½ pts water – bottled rather than tap

The water needs to be chlorine free, either bottled water can be used or add the juice of a lemon to remove the chlorine from tap water. Sterilise the things that will be used if possible. Otherwise, wash them well in very hot water and soap, remember any bacteria that manage to get into the ginger beer may potentially grow and contaminate the batch, spoiling it, remember too, that bacteria are not always friendly.

A large bottle or fermentation vessel is needed to house the ingredients before bottling. Add the lemon juice to the water and put this into the fermentation vessel, add the rest of the ingredients and mix until the sugar has dissolved. Cover the top with muslin to allow air in but keep the bugs out. The more ginger the hotter the ginger beer will be. Leave for a few days at room temperature; try not to let the temperature get to above 85°C. Taste every day, when you bottle this it should be a little sweeter than you would like the finished drink, as it will continue to ferment, reducing the sugar while in the bottle.

To bottle, the equipment should again by scrupulously clean, ideally sterilised. You could use a syphon tube and sieve to transfer the ginger beer to a bottle or pour very carefully through muslin. This will catch the ginger beer plant and stop it ending up in the drink. Try not to disturb any sediment at the bottom of the fermenting vessel.

Put the tops on the bottles and store in a cool place. Unusual though it is, bottles do burst, so check the pressure regularly and release by unscrewing the cap a little if necessary. This is ready to drink when some natural fizz has built up, after about 2-3 days. When it's about right, refrigerate to slow down fermentation but remember this is not a commercial product and will not keep indefinitely.

The ginger beer plant should be saved when it is filtered out and can be reused.

Homemade lemonade

A glass of iced homemade lemonade on a hot summer's day can be very welcome.

> *"Making lemonade became a ritual, the ingredients were laid out, lemons on the tray, sugar next to them, kettle put on to boil and the jug proudly waiting ready on the worktop."*

<u>Quick lemonade</u>
This method can be too bitter for some people's tastes as it includes the pith from the lemons in the preparation, but in its defence, it is very quick.
3 lemons
5oz sugar
1 ½ pints cold water

Blend the lemons, sugar and ½ pint of water in a food processor, blitz until the lemon is finely chopped, but not completely pureed. Put through a sieve, squeezing out as much juice as possible, rinse the flavour out with the rest of the water. Test for sweetness, adding more sugar if needed. Serve over ice.

Lemonade
5 lemons
5oz sugar
2 ½ pints boiling water

Wash the lemons and pare off the rind, put this in a jug with the sugar. Squeeze the lemons and add the juice. Pour the boiling water over the lemon rind and juice, leave to stand until cool, ideally overnight then strain and adjust the sugar. This keeps in the fridge for about a week. Serve with fresh slices of lemon and ice.

Lemon Barley Water

This was a nourishing recipe for invalids and a pleasant summer drink, Nan used to make this in the 1950's and before. Barley water is believed to ease the symptoms of cystitis, but it will not cure it and effects are only temporary. It is also soothing for sore throats and gentle on the digestion. Regularly drinking barley water is said to reduce the risk of kidney stones

Lemon Barley Water

4oz pearl barley
5 lemons
5oz sugar
2 ½ pints boiling water

Rinse the pearl barley under cold running water. Put this in a small saucepan with enough cold water to cover to a depth of about 1". Bring to the boil then simmer for 3 minutes. Strain the liquid off the barley and rinse. Put the barley back in the pan; add the zest and juice of the lemons and the sugar. Pour the boiling water over and leave in a cool place overnight. Strain and store in a cool place.

Lemon Barley Water No Sugar

2 lemons – juice and peel only
¾ cup pearl barley
1 cup of honey
6 cups of water

This recipe substitutes honey for sugar, this also makes it ideal for those with sore throats or respiratory infections. Rinse the pearl barley until the water runs clear. Place the lemon peel and the barley in a pan, add the water, bring to the boil, then turn down the heat and simmer for 15 minutes. The water should be strongly fragranced with lemon; this could simmer for another fifteen minutes for a stronger flavour. Strain and discard the barley. Add the honey and the lemon juice and stir to mix. Refrigerate. Brown sugar, maple syrup or sliced ginger could be added for a change.

The honey could be replaced with a cup of sugar for those who don't like the taste of honey. Grapefruit, lime or oranges could be used to give different flavour or a combination of these. Leftover barley can be used to make a breakfast dish.

Plain Barley Water

This is said to help bring down a fever.

2oz Barley
1 ½ pts water

Bring the water and barley to the boil, turn down the heat and simmer for ten minutes. Strain, pushing out as much of the liquid as you can. Drunk warm it is good for sore throats. Refrigerate until needed.

Cordials

These are a good way of using up excess fruit. Blackberry, blackcurrant, raspberry and rhubarb cordials all work well and are so simple to make. The general principals are the same as for the recipes below, extract the flavour, remove the fruit, boil the juice with sugar, sugar is a preservative and boiling for ten minutes helps to kill bacteria that would spoil the cordial, bottle.

Elderberry cordial

Another common hedgerow tree hosts a profusion of cream coloured, scented flowers in spring and laden with clusters of shiny, black berries hanging like bunches of grapes in the autumn. These are ideal for jam, wine or cordial. Rich in vitamin A, B_6, and C, together with all manner of antioxidants and minerals, the cordial provides a boost to the immune system with the onset of winter. A rich purple, it looks divine in the glass, dilute with hot or cold water. Good in cocktails too. With so many uses for elderberries, it is a good thing they are so quick to pick. Take care though the juice will stain.

2 lbs elderberries
Sugar (brown gives a mellow flavour)
Lemon

Using a fork, strip the elderberries from their stalks straight into a large bowl of cold water, rinse these, discard any that float and any bugs you find! Strain and put the berries in a saucepan. Add enough water to just cover the berries and simmer very gently for about twenty minutes until these are soft and the water deep purple. Strain this, keep the liquid, and push the berries through a sieve to collect as much juice as possible. Measure the juice and for each ½ pint of juice add 8oz sugar and the juice of half a lemon. Bring to the boil and boil for ten minutes, then transfer into sterilised bottles and seal. This should keep well in the fridge, certainly over the winter in unopened bottles. Cinnamon sticks could be added with the sugar and simmered with the fruit, along with ginger if desired.

Blackcurrant cordial

10oz sugar
15oz black currants

Juice of 1 lemon

Method as above

Rosehip Cordial

A delightfully orange-red, syrupy and slightly cloudy cordial. Scarlet wild rosehips stand out against bare hedgerows in autumn and winter packed with vitamin C, collect them when the hips have been softened by frost. A teaspoon of the cordial each morning is reputedly good for fending off winter coughs and colds, but also used as a flavouring for cakes or yoghurt.

2lb wild rosehips
1 lb sugar

Wash the rose hips, then top and tail them, removing any old flowers that may still be attached. Chop finely; you could use a food processor for this. Use only whole, unblemished hips. Place in a large pan and cover with a pint and a half of boiling water, add a little more if this does not cover the hips. Bring back to the boil and boil for two minutes then turn off the heat and leave them to steep for half an hour. Tip into a jelly bag and allow to drain through, when the liquid has stopped dripping out, return the rosehips to the pan and repeat the process using another pint of water or more if necessary. Throw away the pulp. Add another half a pint of water to the syrup and the sugar, bring to the boil and boil for ten minutes. Bottle in sterilised bottles, store in a cool dark place for up to three months although the flavour will quickly decrease.

Once opened this does not keep well, a week or so in the fridge, no more, so use small bottles. Alternatively, this can be stored in the freezer.

Black Country Snowball

Not actually sure this one is pure Black Country, but that was definitely where I was introduced to it and since that day it has become an integral part of Christmas.

If offered a drink when you're out visiting relatives, what do you choose? Something tame you think, nothing too strong. Whisky - no, brandy - no. How about a snowball - perfect. How about a snowball made with just a drop of lime cordial, it had to be Roses lime juice. Advokaat, of course, you can't make a snowball without Advokaat. Add a splash of brandy then top up with Babycham and a cherry. Perfect, yes; but tame most definitely not! I still make it that way now. Thank you, Uncle Reg

Tea

"Mug of strong tea and a packet of Woodbines to start the day"

No recollection of Black Country food and drink would be complete without tea. There was always tea, proper stewed black tea made from leaves, not bags, which were stored in a squat tea caddy, measured out with a square, silver caddy spoon. There was always a pot of tea brewing, no matter what time of day, a pot was always on the go, left on a low light on the stove top to keep it warm for hours in its metal teapot, the kitchen always fragrant with the smell of stewed tea, getting stronger through the day.

Boiling water
Loose tea
Milk and sugar – optional

Run the water, freshly drawn water has more oxygen, which makes for a better taste and only boil it once. Pour a little hot water into the pot to warm it and allow it to stand for a few minutes as the water for the tea boils. Empty the water out of the pot. Use loose tea adding one teaspoonful per cup and one extra for the pot. Pour the boiling water over the tea, put the lid on the pot and put on a tea cosy.

Leave the tea to brew, some teas take longer than others, allow four to five minutes on average, generally the smaller the leaf the more quickly it will brew.

The cups should be fine china for the best experience and be used with a saucer, but failing that, a pot mug will do just fine. Tradition dictates the milk should be added first. This dates back to the days when tea was served in bone china cups; these could represent a considerable investment to a household. Milk in the cup would cool the tea as it was poured in, lessening the likelihood of the cup cracking because of the heat. Sugar, if used was added last.

Once brewed the tea was poured through a tea strainer to catch the leaves.

In times gone by, the custom was to pour the hot tea into the saucer and drink from that, cooling the liquid sufficiently so it did not scald the drinker. These old-fashioned saucers were deeper than their modern equivalents.

That's it – a perfect cup of tea

Mulled Cider

"Grandad was a cider drinker, on occasion, possibly when the weather was cold or around Christmas time he would modify his quaffage to mulled cider. Being tiny at the time, I was most impressed by his method of heating the drink which involved heating the poker in the fire until it was glowing, then plunging the tip into his pewter mug, the spitting and hissing of the aggrieved liquid did much to burn the memories in place."

Cider
Brown sugar
6 Cloves
2 Cinnamon sticks
Red-hot poker optional

Slices of orange

Heat the cider in a pan with the cinnamon sticks, cloves and enough sugar to sweeten, honey could be used in place of the sugar. Add the orange slices and serve. Often a measure of spirits is added before serving to replace the alcohol boiled off. Take care; once brandy has been added this is stronger than it sounds, the alcohol is absorbed more quickly from the hot liquid.

Beer

The author has never brewed beer, not from scratch. But there is a lasting memory of being a very little girl standing in the garden with grandma on a sunny day and looking up at the green hops against a blue sky. The hops had not yet reached to tops of the thin grey wires they were scaling but still, they seemed to climb all the way to the sky. On asking Granny what they were, the answer was hops. “They’re for making beer,” she said. The small dark Brewhouse was often busy.

The papery flowers from the hop bines impart the bitter flavour to the beer, generally, hops are dried, but in wet brewing, the flowers can be used fresh, straight from the bine. Hops would be spread out in the brewhouse after harvest, but there is no recollection of how these were used.

There is a short window for the best flavour to be obtained and if the beer is brewed using fresh hops, these should be harvested from the bines and used straight away, within 24 hours wherever possible. They will not keep. If they cannot be used straight away, they should be dried. From vague memories, the author believes the hops were used dried; the feel of the papery flowers lingers in the memory, but not the process of the brewing.

As with using fresh herbs, the quantities needed can be difficult to gauge. Experience would have played a huge part, but as a rule of thumb, bearing in mind the much higher water content of fresh produce, about 6 – 8 times as many fresh hops would be used in comparison to dry. There is also a risk using wet hops that the fresher flavour will be too prominent in the finished beer. You can even mix wet and dry hops to add to the confusion.

A hop pillow though is used to aid sleep; the dried hops would be tucked inside a pillowcase to release the soporific fragrance to lull the sleeper.

Black Country folk were tough, anyone still standing didn't need a doctor. Old wives tales and home store cupboard remedies abounded, ensuring people did indeed remain standing.

Many older folk will remember the smell of gas tar as roads were repaired. Inhaling the fumes was thought to ease chest infections. "Breathe in," mothers told their children as they walked past the roadworks. A trip to the gas works achieved the same ends, particularly when whooping cough was suspected.

Steam inhalations cleared the tubes. Friar's balsam or a spoonful of Vick dissolved in a bowl of boiling water. Essential oils work almost as well, eucalyptus oil or menthol. The afflicted would lean towards a steaming bowl, cover the head and the bowl with a towel to trap the vapours, then breathed deeply in the steamy atmosphere.

Steam treatment was also used for some types of croup, taking the baby into a bathroom full of steam or leaving the kettle on the hob to boil away moistening the air in the kitchen.

Invalid food

Dishes such as beef tea and egg custard were designed to nourish the invalid, nutritious and light, they would not lie heavy on the stomach of those who were ill or recuperating, quite unlike the food served in hospitals today.

<u>Beef tea</u>

This was believed to contain lots of "goodness" to sustain the invalid. It was what it said, a tea made of beef. Some recipes result in a weak, semi-cooked beef broth. Proper beef tea should be reminiscent of distilled essence of beef. It may not look appealing but generations swore by beef tea to build up those recovering from an illness, don't knock it until you've tried it.

½ lb beef lean beef
3 cups water
Pinch of salt

Add the salt to the water, put in the beef and bring to the boil, turn down the heat and simmer for between 30 minutes and three-quarters of an hour. Skim of any fat and strain. You should be left with a clear brown liquid. There is relatively little nourishment but it is easy on the digestion, will keep the invalid hydrated, it may even stimulate the appetite. For patients who are really struggling to recover, you could double the amount of beef. A carrot and an onion could be added to the water during boiling for more flavour.

Strong beef tea

½ lb lean beef, trimmed of all sinew and gristle
1 ½ cups water

Trim the beef of fat and gristle, then flash fry quickly to brown; you could add a clove of garlic. Cut into small pieces and place in a Kilner jar, use some of the water to deglaze the pan and add this to the jar with the beef. Add the rest of the water and fit the lid. Allow to stand for half an hour, and then place in a pan of cold water. Turn on the heat and slowly bring up to a simmer, do not allow to boil, cook for two hours. This could be left it in the bottom oven of an Aga or Rayburn overnight or in a slow cooker on low for several hours. Cool, strain, remove as much liquid from the beef as possible. Add salt to taste and a squeeze of lemon. Contains plenty of iron, so this is good for post-op recovery or post childbirth.

Junket

Another example of invalid food is junket. Soft to eat and made from wholesome milk, possibly flavoured with honey. Adding rennet to the milk part digests it, making it easier on the stomach. The watery whey is also nutritious and equally good for convalescents.

Egg and Milk

A whole egg and a teaspoon of sugar whisked into half a pint of warm milk, served vaguely cappuccino like with a froth of fine bubbles on the top, was a popular way of tempting poorly children. The taste is fine aged two or three, but the very thought of raw egg and milk now is enough to turn the stomach.

Preventatives

There were regularly administered preparations designed to keep the illnesses at bay, emerging from the bathroom cabinet at the same time as the first frosts. As a small child, the start of winter would be heralded by the appearance of a small flat bottle of blush pink liquid. A teaspoonful of Delrosa Rosehip syrup was given every morning by mothers to their children to keep colds away. Rose-coloured and syrupy sweet, the taste was far too pleasant for something supposed to do you good. Rosehips are rich in vitamins A, C, D and E, which was a major selling point.

Though initially high, the levels of vitamin C would possibly have suffered during the production process. Sadly, this is no longer available in the UK but possibly still on sale in the USA. Should you want to try making rosehip syrup a recipe is given below. Wait until after the first frost before collecting rosehips. The syrup can also be used to flavour cakes or stirred through yoghurt.

Rosehip syrup

4 ½ pts water
2lbs rosehips
1 1/4lbs sugar

Put a pan containing 3 pints of water on to boil while mincing the rosehips, these will be full of fine hairs, which will be itchy if allowed to get into the clothing. Put the minced rosehips straight into the water, the vitamins will begin to breakdown as soon as the hips are broken up, which is why they must go into the water immediately. Boil, and then allow this to settle for 15 minutes before running through a jelly bag. Return the minced rosehips to the pan and add the remaining water, bring to the boil again, allow to settle for a further 15 minutes, then transfer this to the jelly bag and allow it to run through. Filtering through filter paper (coffee filter) will take much longer, leave overnight, but will give a clearer result.

Pour the filtered liquid into a clean pan, there should be no hairs or bits of rosehip evident. Boil and reduce to about 1 ½ pts of liquid. Add the sugar, boil rapidly for 5 minutes and bottle in sterilised bottles, seal. Use small bottles as once opened the syrup will not keep for very long.

"I'm not convinced this helped keep colds away when I was little, but the love that went into doling out those spoonfuls stays with me."

And more…

A teaspoon of malt and cod-liver oil was also prescribed every day, dark, unctuous and treacly, so thick it had to be wound around the spoon, another weapon in the fight against seasonal coughs and colds. The sweet and malty taste disguised the cod liver oil hidden within. Pure malt is still available, without cod liver oil, great for malt loaves, but the price is a bitter pill now. The taste, however, still lovely. Cod liver oil alone, a resounding yuk!!!

Sipping lemon barley water eased a sore throat; the barley gave a silky quality and the lemon, vitamin C.

Hop pillows for insomnia

The soporific, sleep-inducing properties of hops have been understood for centuries. A completely natural remedy, so there are none of the lingering effects associated with sleeping tablets. There is no need to stuff an entire pillow with hops; a few sewn into a muslin bag or placed inside the pillowcase will be enough to release the scent that induces sleep. Sound too good to be true? Cannot hurt to try it if sleep is difficult to find.

One word of caution, although dogs are unlikely to eat hops due to the bitter taste, try to keep the two apart. Hops are toxic to dogs; they are not good for cats either, so if you have pets make sure they do not have access to hops, fresh, dried or in a pillow.

Coughs, colds and other seasonal lurgies

Sore throats

TCP: There was the recommended use as an antiseptic, then there was the other use, gargling neat TCP for a sore throat. No so good when someone slaps the gargler soundly on the back mid-event.

Lemon barley water: Sipped to ease a sore throat; the barley gave a silky quality and the lemon, vitamin C. Honey could be added to sweeten which is a natural antiseptic.

Sniffing the carbolic soap and goose grease rubbed on the chest for colds were also believed to help a cold.

Food followed the seasons, marking the changes through the year. Green asparagus spears poked out above the soil in May, no earlier and not much later. Growing seasons were short. Fresh produce wasn't available on supermarket shelves all year round, imported from far-flung parts of the globe. There was no Sainsbury's when I was young, there wasn't much asparagus about either, not in our house.

Raspberries appeared in the autumn, dried fruits in the winter. A glut of preserving followed the harvest ensuring whatever was grown did not go to waste. Jars of pickles lined up ready for the pantry; onions, red cabbage, damsons, all preserved for the winter, rows of jars of jam on the shelves. Home grown, home cooked, good honest food, a little went a long way.

Times have changed since then. Strawberries from abroad whatever the month were still a generation away. An apple, an orange and a handful of nuts filled the bottom of the Christmas stocking and pink sugar mice with string tails or sugar pigs poked out of the top.

Traditions in the Black Country were similar to those throughout Great Britain, mince pies at Christmas, Hot Cross Buns at Easter; each housewife tweaked the recipes slightly adding their own personal twist. Trifle was always present at full on family gatherings and at the first hint of well-to-do visitors for tea, many folks of a certain era will remember the sound of tins being opened, as John West or Princes salmon left the larder to fill sandwiches, accompanied by thinly sliced onion and/or cucumber bathed in vinegar. Afters would be tinned fruit, peaches or pears (in syrup naturally) and tinned evaporated milk, Carnation milk in the distinctive red and white tin.

Chicken was in real terms, much more costly to buy than it is today; meaning it was reserved for occasions rather than standard Sunday roasts, a "special meal." Capons were for Easter and Christmas. Turkeys were rare, once-a-year-fare, only eaten at Christmas, and in the days leading up to the great event, the birds would appear hanging in rows outside butchers' shops, strung by the necks, still wearing their black and white feathers. Sometimes they would be kept at home in readiness for the big day, suspended from the bannisters waiting to be plucked. Rag and bone men would exchange clothes for tiny chicks as they did their rounds, fluffy yellow balls to be raised at home, but often the poor things did not survive.

Sunday Roasts were an occasion, served with all the trimmings. Yorkshire pudding and horseradish sauce with beef, stuffing and apple sauce with pork. Obligatory roast potatoes with both. Roasting potatoes was a serious business, par-boil the potatoes first for a light and fluffy inside, but the outside must be crisp and golden. Placed around the meat in the roasting tin, these would be basted during cooking and turned at least once, ensuring the outside roasted to perfection. Dripping was (and remains) the ideal roasting medium. Goose fat may be fashionable but leaves a greasy aftertaste and does not have the superior flavour of dripping.

Lamb should be paired with mint sauce to cut through the greasiness and accompanied by the first of the spring vegetables, sweet peas, tiny broad beans and tender, small new potatoes boiled with a sprig of mint.

And there was gravy, lashings of gravy. And pudding, always pudding.

Sunday and other teas

Following Sunday lunch was tea, afternoon tea or high tea was an occasion in itself, lace doilies, linen tablecloths and china, not the best china, not unless there were visitors. The order was pot mugs in the week, china for Sunday tea - but only the second set, bone china for special visitors, the vicar or the mother-in-law. Tea in china cups, brewed in a proper pot, milk in the jug, sugar in the bowl, bottles and jars banished to the kitchen and a starched linen cloth.

There was a certain atmosphere to Sunday tea, especially "special" tea, good manners and formality prevailed. Children were on their best behaviour, "please and thank you" and "please may I leave the table?" were the rule.

In my 1960's childhood, tea was served in the dining room, where in winter a roaring, open coal fire warmed the room, covering the walls with a flickering orange glow. Background music came from a large, valve radio in a wooden case on the shelf. This gave a lovely a mellow tone to the escaping voices that still carried a "BBC accent."

Laid out on the table would be sandwiches, salad, pickles, cake and tinned fruit with Carnation evaporated milk, complemented by thin cut bread and butter, sliced from an uncut loaf by a knife worn narrow from being sharpened many times over the years. The trick to was to butter the bread before slicing, otherwise the act of spreading butter (remember this was in the days before "spreadable straight from the fridge spreads" had come about,) would rip holes in the delicate slices.

Salmon, tinned again, was reserved for special visitors, when the single tin would be opened in honour, all traces of bone painstakingly removed, before mashing the fish with vinegar. There would be sliced onion and cucumber in vinegar or homemade piccalilli to go with the sandwiches. Now and then to ring the changes there were egg sandwiches instead. The eggs were hardboiled and chopped with salad cream or sliced in a peculiar wire contraption. Other variations on the sandwich theme were tongue or ham, sometimes with a salad and beetroot to stain the bread purple. Woe betide anyone who dripped beetroot vinegar on the tablecloth, grandma could be a fearsome beast once riled.

Each item on the table had its own particular dish or bowl, tinned fruit in the serving bowl with the crinoline lady pattern, onion in vinegar in the small, shallow Pyrex dish, trifle in the clear glass bowl. Blue cups and saucers for family, red and gold for visiting family, Old Country Rose pattern for the vicar and other dignitaries.

In pride of place on the table was a glass cake stand covered with a white paper doily on which sat the cake. A cake for cutting, a substantial cake. Fruit cake, Madeira cake, Cherry Cake, good old Victoria sponge, but never, not in our house, Seed Cake. Dad complained the seeds got under his plate.

When the Ladies (they were deserving of a capital L) came together, it was a blend of Macbeth and Last of the Summer wine, best china rattling and tongues clacking, all eyes on the fattest slice of cake.

Victoria Sandwich

8oz butter
8oz sugar
8oz flour
2 eggs
Raspberry jam

Cream the butter with the sugar until light and fluffy, gradually beat in the egg, sift in the flour and cut in with a wooden spoon, try not to knock the air out. Split between two greased 8" sandwich tins, level the tops of these with a spatula and bake in a preheated oven at 350°F, 180°C or Gas Mk 4 for around 20 minutes, until well risen and springy to the touch. Turn out and cool on a wire rack. When cool spread one-half with jam and sandwich the two halves together. A layer of buttercream could also be added. Sprinkle the top with caster sugar before placing with the respect it deserves onto the cake plate.

Birthdays

Children's birthdays were often marked with a party at home, games such as pin the tail on the donkey, pass the parcel and blind man's buff were followed by a laden table of brightly coloured sugar heavy treats. The cake would be carried in; candles blazing and happy birthday iced in scrawling letters across the top, a big breath then make a wish. After all that hard work, the cake would be carved into slices, wrapped in a paper serviette and crammed into a party bag with sweets and assorted plastic gifts, to emerge squashed at the other end. For the younger children, there was often the blancmange rabbit, resplendently resting on green jelly grass.

What the visitors had not seen was the pink puddle on the kitchen table from when the rabbit mould fell over. In the 1960's these were made of very light aluminium and shockingly unstable. Propped upside down with only two spindly antenna shaped stalks at the head end to keep the wretched thing balanced. Full of hot blancmange they were ridiculously top heavy and were toppled the minute your back was turned by the gentlest breeze, releasing the contents all over the kitchen, it was a wonder any rabbits emerged at all.

Trying to entice them out of the mould intact was an art form in itself. Nevertheless, there they would be, every birthday for years, a pink set blancmange in the perfect shape of a rabbit, nestled into that bed of chopped green jelly. Aren't mothers wonderful?

No party would have been complete without inch long cocktail sausages, finger-burningly hot from the oven, twisted from full-size versions the night before. Potatoes wrapped in tin foil transformed into hedgehogs, spiked with cocktail sticks proudly bearing a lump of cheddar and a pineapple chunk. Food of the gods indeed.

Picnics

In the summer, there would be picnics; moisture from the damp grass in the countryside would seep up through the blanket on which the picnic was spread. Sand from the beach managed to work its way over the rug and into the contents of every sandwich in the yellow-lidded Tupperware box. Picnics were always an affair of state, wicker hamper ceremoniously packed and a flask of tea for the journey, consumed later stewed and well past its best from slightly faded red plastic cups. The aroma of egg sandwiches in a warm car is something not to be missed.

Bonfire night

Every village, school or pub had its own bonfire, potatoes baked in the ashes, hot soup and a handful of fireworks. Boxes of fireworks, Brocks or Standard, made their way back to homes in the days before the big night, full of Catherine wheels, roman candles, screech owls and jumping jacks. Children would roam the streets, with a guy made from old clothes, stuffed with straw, paper or old tights, chanting "penny for the Guy," then watching their work consumed by the flames of the fire on November 5th as they wrote their names with sparklers in the dark. Next morning, the smell of smoke would be heavy in the air.

Groaty pudding was customarily served on bonfire night to keep the cold out.

Bonfire toffee

Bonfire night cannot go by, even now, without homemade bonfire toffee, a taste firmly rooted in childhood, the warm glow of blazing fires and the warmth of family. The recipe dates back years, my mother made it, her mother made it and I believe her mother before. For the recipe to have been in use that many years, it must be good!

During WW2, my mother, who was only young then and a brown owl in the girl guides, was at a residential camp. Enough sugar and butter coupons had been collected to make two tins of bonfire toffee over the campfire.

Later, after everyone had retired to bed, the toffee was left outside to set ready for the morning. Mum was woken with a start in the wee small hours. Outside the tent, there was a rustling and a snuffling. Wild beasts had stormed the camp and the guides were in her charge. She could hear breathing in the inky darkness, as she peeled back the opening of the tent a crack. Heart hammering she peered through the gap. The dying embers of the fire flickered red in the eyes of the beast. Outside a hedgehog was standing in the tin feasting on their toffee! At least the other tin was saved.

Below is Nana's recipe for that same toffee.

8oz butter
1 small tin condensed milk
3 tablespoons golden syrup
12oz sugar
1 tablespoon vinegar – mum used ordinary malt vinegar

Melt the butter gently in a pan, stir in the sugar, mixing occasionally so the sugar doesn't form lumps, dissolve the sugar completely then bring to the boil. Add the other ingredients boiling up after each one. Mum used to add malt vinegar to help prevent the formation of crystals, these days I tend not to do this. Lemon juice could be substituted instead. Finally, boil for ten minutes, the colour will turn rich brown and the bubbles will change as the toffee nears temperature. Keep a saucer close by with an ice cube to test for the set. If the toffee sets on the cold saucer, it's done, alternatively use a sugar thermometer and aim for the soft crack stage. Pour into greased tins and leave to set. The longer you boil the toffee the firmer the set will be, so if you like softer, chewier toffee, aim for chestnut, conker brown will be harder.

Christmas

A special magical time before the days when it was dominated by money, turning into the consumer-fest it is now. Religion still mattered, and family. The true meaning of Christmas was remembered. That said, presents were always welcome.

Letters would be written and thrown up the chimney for Father Christmas, presents wrapped and hidden. The tree was decorated with tinsel and multi-colour paper chains hung from the bannisters. That same fairy sat on top of that tree every year for my entire childhood.

On Christmas Eve, stockings would be hung on the fireplace or put on the end of the bed, mince pies and a glass of whisky for Father Christmas and a carrot for Rudolph, left on the hearth. I would give so much for to go back for one last family Christmas.

Brandy Butter

"There had to be brandy butter at Christmas and a white rum sauce to go on the pudding. But the brandy butter was always leftover in the fridge after Christmas, one of those essentials that no-one ever ate."

4oz butter, softened
2oz light muscovado sugar
4oz icing sugar, sieved
3 tablespoons brandy or cognac

Cream the butter until soft, beat in the sugars then slowly add the brandy. This can be done in a food processor. If the butter splits when the brandy is added, beat in a little more icing sugar until it is smooth again. Store in the fridge and serve with Christmas puddings or mince pies.

Mince pies

Pastry – see earlier
Mincemeat – see recipe in preserve section
Icing sugar – to sprinkle

Roll the pastry thinly on a floured board. Select two pastry cutters, one slightly smaller than the other. Grease a tartlet tin, then cut an equal number of bases (larger size) and tops (smaller size cutter). Place a base in each hole in the tin, add a spoonful of mincemeat, top with a lid and press the edges to seal. Bake in a moderate oven until the pastry is coloured. Remove from the tin and cool on a rack, decorate with sifted icing sugar.

Christmas pudding

This needs to be made in advance giving time for the flavours to mature. The last Sunday before Advent was given the name Stir up Sunday and this was the traditional day set aside for making Christmas pudding. A family affair, ideally every member of the family would have been present for the making. They would give it a stir and make a wish for the coming year, a huge help to the cook, puddings are heavy to mix.

The name for the day actually derives from a line in the Book of Common Prayer "Stir up, we beseech thee, O Lord, the wills of thy faithful people," but has been hijacked by pudding makers up and down the land, including the Black Country.

Every family has a pudding recipe handed down, this doesn't mean it's made every year or every five years, or even ten but that little piece of history is still there, hidden away in some handwritten cookery book in the bottom of a drawer, linking the generations.

This was mums. The recipe book is from the 1960's, well-worn

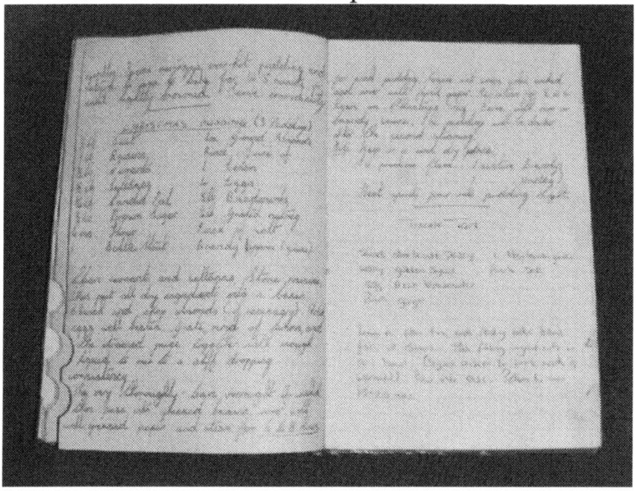

now, the spine has split and grease marks are evident on some of the pages. Another that predates it was probably begun in the '30's. Mum is no longer here to ask about cooking times or ingredients, but her recipes are. This one is tweaked every time it is made, the quantity of brandy has been increased significantly, and the stout is generally replaced, orange substituted for lemon, a few cherries thrown in, but it is still mum's recipe, and she's there, in my memory every single time it's made.

A good pudding had to make an entrance, flaming the pudding is almost akin to piping in the haggis, dim the lights for full effect as the pudding is carried with pride to the dining room, clothed in blue flames. It's a simple thing to flame a pudding as long as a few rules are followed:

1. The pudding should be stinking hot – in these days of technology nuke it in the microwave for 30 seconds.
2. Sprinkle a tablespoon of good old white sugar over the top before pouring over the alcohol. The flames will caramelise this as they burn and the smell as they do…
3. Nuke the alcohol. This needs to be warm too
4. Pour one over the other, add flame, and there you have it. A flaming pudding.

Don't forget the tanner (sixpence) in the pudding. Previously to this, a silver threepenny bit or silver charm was used. At home it was always put in after steaming, an old-fashioned sixpence, but traditionally this was stirred into the mix and cooked in the pudding. Whoever found it on Christmas day was assured wealth and good luck in the coming year. Some years it was a monopoly counter, a thimble or the top hat. These always magically reappeared, all trace of pudding removed, in the monopoly set later

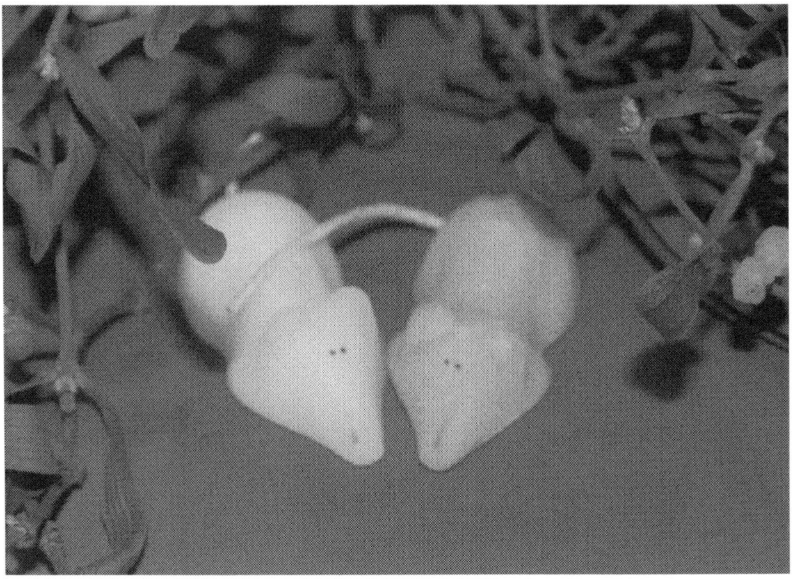

And Finally…

"My Gran had a lock up Fish shop in Bridge Street, Coseley up until the 50s. She used to buy great big slabs of beef lard. From what I can remember, these were put in a huge copper with a wood fire underneath. She made the batter herself. It would just have been plain ingredients, because there was nothing else then. Mom used to have to fetch the fish in an old pram from Bilston, which she hated. Also, we had a potato peeler in the back yard. The eyes were taken out by hand. Really hard work, day in day out. I don't know how long Gran had it for, but it would have been the early 1900s. After she retired she would cook chips at home, they would be dark brown and lovely and soft in the middle." Catherine Flavell

No book about food in the Black Country would be complete without a mention of that staple of the Midlands diet, fish and chips. Fifty years ago, there was a fried fish shop on almost every street corner, now they are not so plentiful and the contents far more varied representing the global market. Curry sauce (often a choice of types) sold in polystyrene pots in addition to mushy peas, there are kebabs with lemon juice and chilli sauce or vegetarian options but always good old-fashioned fish in batter remains in pride of place on the menu.

Fish and chips emerge crisp and hot from a seething, boiling bath of bubbles, but no longer fried in lard or beef dripping, the cooking medium also updated, replaced with a vat of oil. The batter itself has also changed, more orange and thicker than the thin, red-brown coating remembered from youth.

Shiny tiles lined the shop walls, heat from the frying range warmed the counter, customers would snuggle closer in the winter as they queued to be served, an antidote to the foul weather outside. Later the package wrapped in day old newspapers would warm the fingers on the journey home.

A jar of white pickled eggs standing proudly on the counter and hubbly bubbly pop to drink from a glass bottle decorated with bubble shapes set into the top half.

You could ask for batter bits with your chips, this was the excess batter that came off the fish during the cooking process, sometimes you could strike gold and find a piece of fish in the bits. Few chip shops seem to make this common knowledge now, perhaps with the today's batter they are not so plentiful, or perhaps it's a well-guarded trade secret.

But a taste of that past is still available at the Black Country Museum, fish and chips as they used to be, fried in dripping with batter bits.

I can almost smell the vinegar.

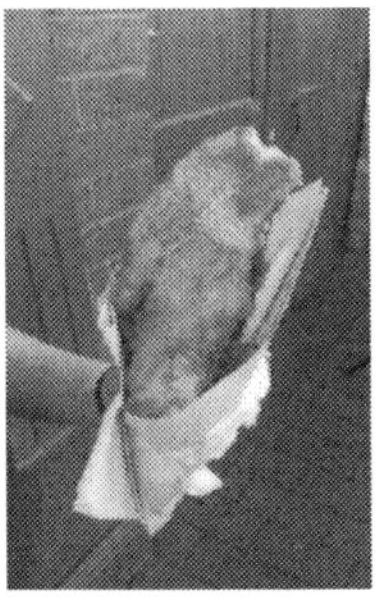

Butchers and bakers delivering to the back door, peeling back the cloth of the huge wicker basket to reveal the differently shaped loaves below. Milk – gold top delivered fresh to the door every day with thick yellow cream on top. Sawdust on the butcher's floors to catch the blood as it dripped from the carcasses. Keeping the milk cold in a bowl of water in the summer

Milk delivered by electric float and before that by horse and cart

Sweets brought in quarters or ounces weighed out from big glass jars poured from the scale scoop into paper bags. Cheese cut with a wire, not strangled in plastic.

Bread wrapped in white tissue paper, chips in newspaper. Bottles wrapped in sometimes coloured, often white tissue from the offie

Loose tea wrapped into quarters in oblong paper packages

Collecting tea cards and brook bond orange stamps. Green shield stamps

Clean your plate or dinner served up again for tea. May I leave the table? No bottles or jars on the table

Corona pop in glass returnable bottles, milk bottles rushing past the window in the dairy on the Penn Rd (Midland Dairy)

Red lion eggs, butter from a slab, shaped with wooden spatulas, milk delivered by churn, ladled out into your jug. Possible to buy it still warm from the cow in the country, tasted completely different, never tried it but mum loved it

Sugar and salt in blocks. Wrapped in waxed paper about the same size as a sliced loaf today. Salt carved off a big block by the grocer in the shop, grated down at home or delivered by horse and cart in Gornal. Smashed up into smaller pieces on the table with a flat iron. Salt and a lump of coal taken to a new house for luck

Worms in apples. Cutting mars bars into slices. End of rationing in the 50's

Bacon sliced to order, proper bacon without the water, greenback

Pencil tucked behind the ear, figures jotted down on scraps of paper and the bill totted up. No automatic cash registers

Travelling to the countryside in summer for a hop-picking holiday. At harvest time, horse-drawn carts would bring labourers into help. Some of these workers were itinerant gypsies.

In a generation, things have changed, times moves on.

Breweries in pubs, Ma Pardoes, Beacon hotel. Pubs being pubs, serving beer not food, a meeting place.

Simple, cheap nutritious food

Stew jars, black lead, cooking ranges, Dutch ovens, mountains of washing up done by hand.

Tapioca, urghh, used to sneak it onto the plate next to you, to wrap it in a hankie to fool the dinner ladies.

Square cornets for brick ice cream, we used to bite the bottom off and suck the ice cream through. Lovely

Making a gingham apron in needlework and using it in cookery lessons. Everything was crammed into a wicker basket to carry it all, the ingredients never fit in.

Cream horns filled with Sympathetic cream

Frogspawn sago, transparent, tasteless grey blobs

On a Sunday mum could take a beautiful piece of meat and turn it into a lump of charcoal

Poking a knife into steak and kidney pud and watching the gravy run out

Sticky trotter fingers, fingers would glue themselves together as we ate them

Pig tail and pearl barley soup with bread to dip in

A piece of bread and dripping

Coal fire. Sunday tea. Frog spawn tapioca.

Pigs feet. Pig on the wall. Pigs pudding. Pigs tails

"If you get a pigs head ask the butcher to leave the eyes in so it'll see you through the week."

I say, I say, I say, butcher, do you have a sheeps head?
No, it's just my bushy eyebrows.

Printed in Great Britain
by Amazon

13369805R00119